Approaching the Bible as Literature

Approaching the Bible as Literature

An Interactive Workbook

Thomas Schmidt

APPROACHING THE BIBLE AS LITERATURE
An Interactive Workbook

Copyright © 2016 Thomas Schmidt. All rights reserved. Except for brief quotations in critical publications or reviews, no part of this book may be reproduced in any manner without prior written permission from the publisher. Write: Permissions, Wipf and Stock Publishers, 199 W. 8th Ave., Suite 3, Eugene, OR 97401.

Scripture quotations are from New Revised Standard Version Bible, copyright © 1989 National Council of the Churches of Christ in the United States of America. Used by permission. All rights reserved.

Cascade Books
An Imprint of Wipf and Stock Publishers
199 W. 8th Ave., Suite 3
Eugene, OR 97401

www.wipfandstock.com

PAPERBACK ISBN: 978-1-4982-8155-3
HARDCOVER ISBN: 978-1-4982-8157-7

Cataloguing-in-Publication data:

Schmidt, Thomas.

    Approaching the Bible as literature : an interactive workbook / Thomas Schmidt.

    xvi + 200 pp. ; 23 cm. Includes bibliographical references.

    ISBN 978-1-4982-8155-3 (paperback) | ISBN 978-1-4982-8157-7 (hardback)

    1. Bible—Criticism, interpretation, etc. 2. Bible as literature. I. Title.

BS535 S3 2016

Manufactured in the U.S.A.   04/27/16

Contents

Section One: Before "In the Beginning"

1. Approaching the Bible as Literature: How and Why? | 3
2. From Ancient Stories to NRSV: How We Got Here | 8
3. Truth and truth in the Bible | 13

Section Two: Story and Meaning in Historical Narrative

4. The Past Reveals the Present in Genesis 1–11 | 19
5. Telling the Story Well: Narrative Technique in Genesis and Exodus | 29
6. Narrative from Exodus to Samuel | 38
7. From Solomon to the Close of the Old Testament | 44

Section Three: Poetry, Problems, and Promise in Psalms, Prophecy, and Wisdom

8. Principles of Hebrew Poetry | 49
9. Imagery in Hebrew Poetry | 56
10. From Lament to Praise in the Book of Psalms | 61
11. The Prophets Speak for God | 66
12. Pondering Imponderables in Wisdom Literature | 79

Section Four: The Not-So-Silent Silent Years

13. The View from the Bridge | 95
14. Old Testament Plus | 100

Section Five: Gospel and the Life and Teachings of Jesus

15. One Story, Four Versions | 109
16. Jesus According to Matthew | 116

Section Six: Parable as Invitation to the Kingdom and Discipleship
- **17** Principles of Parables | 135
- **18** Parables of Kingdom and Discipleship | 139

Section Seven: Epistle as Window into the Life of the Early Church
- **19** The Epistle and Community Construction | 147
- **20** A Brief History of Early Christianity | 151
- **21** Style and Content in the Epistles | 154

Section Eight: Apocalyptic and Future Hope in the Book of Revelation
- **22** Apocalyptic and Prophecy in the New Testament | 169
- **23** Image and Message in Revelation | 172
   Summing Up | 181

   Glossary | 183
   For Further Reading | 186
   Index |

Section One

Before "In the Beginning"

Chapter 1

Approaching the Bible as Literature
How and Why?

Belief and Unbelief in the Study of the Bible

How would you complete this sentence from the options listed below? The Bible is . . .

—God's written Word, fully inspired, true in every detail, without error of any kind.

—the Word of God, including some human errors or inconsistencies that do not diminish its unique status as the definitive guide for faith and conduct.

—not quite the Word of God, but it *contains* the Word of God, inspirational nuggets that people may find here and there within it.

—a significant and inspirational collection of writings that merits our study along with the sacred texts of other religions.

—essential for an understanding of Western civilization, ideas, and literature, but not inspired in a religious sense.

—the foundational text for Judaism and Christianity, but not important beyond its significance for the understanding of these religions.

—a boring compilation of doctrine, commandments, and obscure ancient history that I wouldn't read if you paid me.

—a dangerous and potentially divisive book that has influenced some good but has also contributed to sexism, racism, sectarianism, and war.

—a book about which I know so little that I decline to choose one of these options.

—none of the above, but [compose your own response].

It is likely that if you are reading this book for a class with fifteen or more students, at least one of your classmates will check each of these responses. Do you welcome such variety? Do you think that some of the options listed above are terribly wrong? Are you open to changing your own response based on further study? Are you concerned that the text, the teacher, or some of your classmates may have an agenda to influence you? Are these questions beginning to make you uncomfortable? Welcome to diversity of the *mind*—which, unlike other kinds of diversity, may be invisible not only to the naked eye but also to the *inward* eye, because we don't always know what we think ourselves until we think longer and more deeply. Now multiply your own combination of certainties and uncertainties by the number of your fellow students, and you begin to appreciate the almost infinite and ever-changing variety of responses to that seemingly simple question: What is the Bible? To encounter this kind of diversity is to face great challenges—and great possibilities for personal and interpersonal growth.

Several years ago, I was asked to teach a college course on the Bible as literature. Knowing that my students would represent the full spectrum of responses listed above, I looked for a textbook that would be helpful to all. I was frustrated, however, to find book after book that I knew would alienate one or another group of students. Some texts assume Christian readers and even include suggestions for prayer and personal response. Other texts, claiming to be neutral in matters of faith, undermine traditional beliefs by mentioning only the most skeptical views regarding biblical authorship and historical accuracy.

A more inclusive approach is possible. One can gain much from a study of the Bible without belief, and one can take a scholarly approach to the Bible while maintaining a vibrant faith. Why shouldn't a textbook convey sensitivity to the diversity present in most classrooms?

While it may not be possible to write a text that is perfectly neutral, it should be possible to impart useful knowledge with care and respect for students at every point along the spectrum of belief. My classroom experience in both secular and confessional institutions has shown me that students who feel safe and respected engage in healthy dialogue with each other and with the instructor. This safety includes not only the tone of the classroom but also the books that students are assigned to read. Conversely, when groups or individuals perceive that their belief or skepticism is under attack, they become silent, defensive, or even aggressive. If we teachers "play it safe" by pushing personal beliefs out of the classroom, the result is further ignorance and fear among those who differ. The more challenging but more rewarding approach is to engage in open dialogue that neither belittles nor proselytizes.

Is this a hopeless ideal? I do not think so. For some, the Bible inspires passionate conviction and the hope to convert others; conversely, some who reject the Bible's authority are evangelistic about their skepticism. There is a wide range between these two approaches, and no reader comes to this study without some already established opinions and motives. But if we openly acknowledge our assumptions and objectives—yes, including the instructor's—we build trust and tolerance, and ultimately we render our own beliefs more attractive.

Terminology of the Bible

Christians refer to the two parts of their Bible as the Old and New Testaments. By this distinction they mean that God made a *testament* (alternately *covenant* or *agreement*), involving promises and obligations, to establish the Jews as a nation, and this story is developed in the books of the Old Testament. Christians believe, further, that Jesus established a *new* testament to complete the old, and the books that explain this are consequently known as the New Testament. Jews, who for the most part do not consider Jesus their messiah, recognize only the Hebrew Bible (the Christian Old Testament) as *scripture* or inspired writing, and the books are in somewhat different order. Because this text quotes from The New Revised Standard Version of the Bible (NRSV), which follows the Christian sequence of books and refers to the older collection as the Old Testament, I will use that term here. I will also use the traditional designations for date BC (before Christ) and AD (*anno domini,* in the year of our Lord) rather than BCE (before common/Christian/current era) and CE (common/Christian/current era), which often appear in scholarly writings. My choices are merely stylistic: I prefer to use the most familiar terms whenever possible in an introductory-level text.

Who wrote the Bible, and when? This is a matter of great complexity and vigorous debate. The thirty-nine books of the Old Testament were written over many centuries by at least thirty different authors. The twenty-seven books of the New Testament were written from about AD 50–100, and they are attributed to nine different authors. But names are attached to many books by tradition, not by indication in the documents themselves. Even when names are given, questions may arise; as a result, numerous books of the Old Testament and several books of the New Testament are subject to considerable dispute regarding authorship and time of origin.

The Bible is not organized in a strictly chronological sequence. In fact, not all Bibles follow the same order or number of books. Jews, Catholics, and Protestants organize the Old Testament differently; furthermore, some Bibles include an additional group of writings known as the Apocrypha, which only Roman Catholics include in the *canon* (official list of books approved as Scripture). The first part of the Old Testament, Genesis through Kings, is generally chronological. Books containing wisdom, poetry, and prophecy follow and are organized by a mix of tradition and chronology. In the New Testament, the Gospel of Matthew is first by tradition, probably because of its length and close relation to the Old Testament. The Book of Acts follows the four Gospels with a record of the beginnings of Christianity. Next are Paul's letters, organized by length—first to churches, then to individuals. There is no apparent pattern to the sequence of the remaining New Testament letters except that longer letters attributed to Peter and John are followed by their shorter letters, and Revelation is the last book because it describes the end of time.

Why Study the Bible as Literature?

Most of us want to broaden and deepen our understanding of the world and of ourselves. We broaden our understanding by learning how others think and live, not only in our own time but also in times past. We deepen our understanding by exploring ideas and issues that we believe are important. Because the ancient Jewish and early Christian writings have done so much to shape our world, knowledge about them can help both to broaden and to deepen us. Our study of these texts helps us to understand our history, the development of human thought, and the techniques used to convey important ideas.

All of this is useful even apart from issues of personal faith. Some prefer to study the Bible for purely educational reasons independently of its claims to present ultimate truths. Others seek further information about the Bible to help decide for themselves if it is inspired. Still others approach the Bible as believers who hope to find their faith supported and enriched by new perspectives on their sacred texts. All of these agendas can be served by consideration of the Bible as literature.

How can one text be fair to such a diversity of readers? Later in the book, for example, we will examine the effect of communicating the life and teachings of Jesus in story form in four separate Gospels. We will not, however, attempt to determine if Jesus was raised from the dead or if he is humanity's savior. These are important historical and doctrinal questions with potentially life-changing and world-changing implications—but they are beyond the scope of this book. Our concerns will be literary: how do the circumstances of the writers and the techniques they employed work to convey their message? The fact that this is not an "ultimate" question should not diminish the importance of our task. For people of faith, a literary approach to Scripture may reveal God in new ways: perhaps as an artist who works with words just as with sunsets and waterfalls. For those whose interest is simply educational, this literary approach may reveal why these writings have stood the test of time to exert such a great influence on human culture. For those trying to evaluate various truth claims, a literary approach may help to confirm or deny the notion of the Bible as unique or profound. In other words, whatever agenda the reader brings to the Bible, its consideration as literature can serve that agenda.

The Perspective of the Writer

Does it matter to our study if I, as the writer of this textbook, or you its reader, regard the Bible as inspired or as only a book of historical importance? First, it is useful to ask what we mean by *inspired*. To inspire means literally to breathe spirit into something, and most readers would agree that the Bible has a lot of spirit, at least in the sense of exerting influence. But traditionally, the inspiration of the Bible has been understood to mean that God's Spirit "breathed" divine truth into the text to make it a reliable guide for faith and practice. Beliefs about how this "breathing" worked vary, from God practically moving the biblical writers' pens across the pages to writers of faith crafting works that were subsequently recognized as Scripture by the community of faith. Now, it is true that those who grant the Bible unique status also find their faith influenced by other kinds of literature: sermons, hymns, novels, nonfiction books, even film scripts. In this sense, inspiration is present in many places, but without quite the level of authority granted to the Bible. People of faith do not, however, have a corner on the term. Nonbelievers who reject any supernatural element in writing might still use the terms "inspired" or "inspiring" for a literary work that is brilliantly crafted or profoundly insightful. We all read to know that we are not alone, to find wisdom, guidance, and meaning. So whether we regard the Bible as "God-breathed" or read it only for its historical significance, we cannot separate our reading of this or any important work from our search for value and meaning, from our craving for the artful and the profound. In this sense, any reading of the Bible is part of a search for *inspiration*, even if the word is understood in secular terms.

So what of my own beliefs, and why mention them? Every writer or teacher brings a perspective, and the reader should suspect those who claim to be "objective" or "scholarly": common code words for a not-so-hidden agenda. If a writer or teacher is open about personal commitments, students can take those beliefs into account as part of the learning process.

As a Christian, I choose to regard the Bible as a dependable guide to help me live in right relationship with God and with other people. At the same time, I understand that the Bible is complex, written in ancient languages over centuries and containing many difficulties of interpretation that challenge highly trained scholars. I am one of those scholars, but I am also a person in progress. What answers I have found to life's questions I must hold humbly while getting on with my primary task, which is to act in love. Further, I understand that my calling is to be a teacher, not a preacher, which means that I write for all students equally, whatever their beliefs. I expect that all will be challenged by this book; I promise that all will be respected and supported.

How to Use This Book

Before we look into the Bible itself, there are two more helpful topics to consider. In the next chapter, I will offer an outline of the Bible's history, from its origins to our modern English text. Then I will introduce a discussion of the concept of truth, both religious and historical, in relation to sacred writings. From that point, I divide the text into sections, each focused on a kind or *genre* of biblical writing: narrative, poetry, wisdom, gospel, parable, epistle, and apocalyptic. Sections include chapters that explain literary features, historical information, and brief descriptions of biblical books linked to the material considered in that section. Since my organization of the material is roughly chronological, you will discover that *Approaching the Bible as Literature* provides a bare-bones introduction to the content of the Bible and the sweep of events that constitute biblical history.

It is not *information*, however, but *participation* that makes this book potentially valuable. After explaining the historical context and particular literary technique under consideration for that section, the text becomes interactive. I will ask you to read specific biblical texts and respond to a series of questions, with blank space provided for writing. This workbook approach is the key to the book, the element that allows for personal engagement and in-depth thought. If you flip through right now to get a sense of the amount of blank space, you can imagine cutting out that much material from a book that is entirely printed text. That is some measure of the content you would miss by not responding to the questions. Indeed, to the extent that the spaces are filled with your own authentic, thoughtful responses, they constitute the best writing in the book.

Taking This Book Further

The suggestions "for further study" at the end of each chapter involve additional questions, topics, or activities relevant to the material. This feature makes the text like a carry-on suitcase with expansion zipper, enabling the instructor to treat any chapter in greater depth, to turn a one-semester course into two, or to substitute assignments for those in the text. For those interested in further reading or research, I include an appendix that not only lists titles for each chapter but also comments on their theological perspective.

Chapter 2

From Ancient Stories to NRSV
How We Got Here

Keeping Records in Ancient Times

Humans are storytelling animals. We have always told stories, and over time we seem to add more ways to tell them. The little shapes on this page, for example, constitute an amazing code that we humans invented only a few thousand years ago. It is astounding, if you stop to consider, that I can touch these keys knowing that they will eventually encounter your optic nerve and pass into your brain, where you will translate them into images and combine them into stories—almost instantly. With only a few keystrokes, I can transport you to the distant past (pyramids under construction), the future (you playing with your grandchildren), or even to scenes that never were or will be (pink elephants on ice skates). We tell or witness stories constantly—conversations, text messages, sporting events, films, music—and we keep going even while we're asleep in the form of dreams.

The technology for recording our stories probably began with cave paintings, progressed to stone carving, and gained efficiency about five thousand years ago with use of a wooden stylus pressed into soft clay. Later, people began to write on animal skins and plant fibers. Now we rely increasingly on electronic images projected onto screens. But when we consider the development of *permanent* record-keeping, we should remember that people have long conveyed information and stories *orally*. The human memory is, in fact, capable of prodigious feats of data preservation. Even today, for example, orthodox Jewish rabbis commonly memorize the entire Hebrew Bible. Scholars speculate that Homer's great epics were originally spoken from memory and later written during the lifetime of the poet, which happened to be the period when the Greek language first took written form.

Further back, records of great events in families or clans, and stories of origins, were undoubtedly preserved for centuries by faithful recitation. This is not to say that once a story was accepted no changes were ever made; but the power of memory and respect for tradition may help to account for remarkable detail preserved for long periods simply by oral records.

Who Wrote the Story?

When it came time for the ancient Jews to commit to writing stories of their past that were already present in oral form, they left no records of the process. In the nineteenth century, scholars began to ask questions about how these books originated. They had little more to go on than the biblical texts themselves and similar writings from surrounding cultures that may provide hints of how, why, and when these kinds of writings were composed.

The first five books of the Bible, which cover the period from creation to the Jewish people on the brink of invading Israel, are Genesis, Exodus, Leviticus, Numbers, and Deuteronomy. Traditionally these books together are called the *Pentateuch* (Greek: "five books"). There is no author named in these books, but according to Jewish tradition, Moses wrote them. This possibility, however, runs into several objections. Moses, who lived in the fourteenth century BC, wasn't around at creation or at other events described in these books that took place long before his time. So if Moses wrote the books, he had to use previously-existing records—and who wrote those? There are also problems of historical detail that suggest writing much later than the time of Moses.

A range of solutions has been proposed to account for these and other challenges to Mosaic authorship. The most widely-held explanation is the *documentary hypothesis* or *JEDP theory*, which attributes the different distinctive styles of writing in the Pentateuch to four different writers or groups of writers. Scholars designate as *J* those sections that use Jahweh as the name for God, where the style is folksy and tends to give human qualities to God. They designate as *E* those sections where Elohim is the Hebrew name for God; these sections are more epic and formal in style. Genesis 1 is a classic example of an E section; Genesis 2–3 is a J section. Further fine tuning on the part of scholars has isolated two other styles of writing in the Pentateuch. These are the *D* (Deuteronomic) sections, which are sermon-like in style and stress loving and obeying God; and the *P* (Priestly) sections, which include lengthy behavioral codes and details regarding rituals and religious buildings. According to the theory, the four documents were composed and then combined from about 800–450 BC.

Despite its popularity as an explanation for the differences of style within the Pentateuch, the documentary hypothesis has been strongly criticized, and not only by defenders of older traditions. Many scholars, for example, consider the reconstruction of sources an overly speculative endeavor. While they affirm that sources were used, they maintain that the Pentateuch's overall unity of design and strategy of composition points to a single author at some point, and that its purposes are more fruitful avenues of study than its origins. More conservative scholars maintain that at least some of the material could have been preserved from ancient records or composed by Moses himself. For people of faith, the possibility that the process took decades or even centuries does not rule out the notion that God gave inspiration to those involved in the entire process of preservation and writing. From a literary perspective, scholars all across the spectrum of belief agree that the books of the Pentateuch exhibit extraordinary skill in presentation of plot and character. It is these qualities that will form the substance of our study of the texts themselves.

Approaching the Bible as Literature

Creation and Canonization of the Old Testament

The Old Testament itself refers to "the book of the law" in 2 Kings 22–23, when King Josiah begins a religious reform by reading aloud from a sacred text, which scholars believe may have been the book of Deuteronomy. After the Jews returned from exile in the fifth century BC, they rebuilt their temple and began to study "the law" (Nehemiah 7–10). Although the books they studied are not specified, they are probably the books of the Pentateuch.

It is likely that the other history books and most of the prophetic writings were collected with some kind of official status by the end of the fourth century BC. In the Hebrew Bible, these are known as the former and latter prophets, or *Nevi'im*. A third category of writings, the *Ketuvim*, consists of the Psalms, Proverbs, Job, and a few others books; these were written and gained status as scripture over a long period, from the tenth century BC to the first century AD. Together with the books of the law or *Torah* (Pentateuch), the letters for this threefold division form the Hebrew anagram TNK, pronounced and written *Tanakh*, which is another term for the entire Hebrew Bible. This organization by category—history, miscellaneous writings, prophets—explains why the books do not occur quite in order of the events recorded. In the case of the prophets, events pertain to material in the later history books; in the case of the writings, the historical setting is less important given the general nature of the content.

Scholars disagree about the extent of revision that may have taken place in some books after their original composition and when the Tanakh became the official canon of Scripture for the Jews. For the entire collection, the process of composition and revision may span nearly a thousand years. But at some point, the Jews perceived a need to recognize and preserve a particular group of writings as scripture. It is likely that something very close to our Old Testament was in place as early as the second century BC, although the official list of books may not have been fixed until the second century AD. After that, although copying by hand was the only technology available, study of surviving manuscripts confirms that painstaking care was taken to preserve and copy each letter of the sacred texts.

Creation and Canonization of the New Testament

The earliest New Testament documents were letters or *epistles* from first generation leaders like Paul, who were known as *apostles* ("sent ones"). Epistles from apostles, composed beginning about AD 50, carried great authority and were soon copied, circulated, and collected. The Gospels and Acts ("The Acts of the Apostles"), which tell the story of Jesus and the early spread of Christianity, composed as early as AD 60, and they too were copied for distribution. By the early second century many other writings appeared as well, some by later Christian leaders, and some whose authorship, accuracy, or ideas were disputed. In order to preserve the authority of the earliest writings, Christian leaders began to compile "official" lists as early as the middle of the second century. Whereas the Jews included books in the Hebrew canon that they consider prophetically inspired, the Christians based their canon on *apostolicity*: authorship by an apostle or associate. Books excluded from the New Testament include many writings quite consistent with the message of the canonical books but written by later church leaders; other excluded books include numerous apocryphal and pseudepigraphal writings like those associated with the Old Testament.

Determining apostolicity was a matter of some debate, and some New Testament books were disputed because their authorship was in doubt, others because their content was brief or, in the case of Revelation, obscure. Although the bulk of the New Testament books were accepted as authoritative writings almost as soon as they were written, it was not until the end of the fourth century AD that the New Testament canon we know today was made official.

Translating the Bible

Because the Christian message quickly spread throughout the linguistically diverse Roman Empire, translation of the New Testament into other languages began almost immediately. Of course some translation was necessary even before writing the New Testament, since the spoken language of Jesus and his first followers was Aramaic, whereas the New Testament books are written in Greek. The first translations from Greek were probably into Syriac, which is similar to Aramaic; and an early Latin version followed—both of these in the second century AD. Other early translations still valued for their historical significance include Coptic, Georgian, and Gothic versions. By late in the fourth century, Latin had replaced Greek as the language of the Roman Empire, and the scholar Jerome was commissioned to make a new translation of the entire Bible into Latin. This version in the common language of the Roman Empire became known as the *Vulgate* (*vulgar* is Latin for "common"), and eventually it became the official Bible of the Roman Catholic Church.

During the Renaissance in the fifteenth and sixteenth centuries, a renewed interest in the original biblical languages led to new collections and investigations of ancient texts. Even though most people were illiterate, translation of the Bible over the next hundred years into languages like German and English was part of the turmoil of the Reformation. Translators were persecuted at first by religious authorities because they made the Bible available to the common people, which compromised the control of the Church. This was also the period when division of the Bible into chapters and verses occurred; the original biblical texts did not divide between words, much less between chapters and verses.

The confusing multiplication of English translations led King James in 1611 to authorize a group of anonymous scholars (possibly including great poets like John Donne and George Herbert) to produce an Authorized Version, now known as the King James Version (KJV). This beautifully written translation gained status over time, and three hundred years of tradition made it the only possible translation for many. Ongoing study of ancient texts, however, along with the discovery of more ancient manuscripts, resulted in challenges to the supremacy of the KJV. By the nineteenth century, new translations began to appear, and some of these translations have been updated over time based on further study and the need to update the English style; for example, the American Standard Version (ASV, 1901) became the Revised Standard Version (RSV, 1952) and then the New Revised Standard Version (NRSV, 1989), the translation used in this textbook.

The Bible has now been translated into more than 2500 languages, but by far the greatest variety—and controversy—occurs in the dozens of English translations. This variety reflects not only debate about style and content but also effective marketing by publishers. Some of the choice between versions falls along denominational lines. For example, Roman Catholics generally use the New Jerusalem Bible (NJB, 1985), and the most popular version among evangelical Protestants is the New International

Version (NIV, 1978, 2011). The KJV is still widely used among conservative groups, and there is also a popular New King James Version (NKJV, 1982) which is based on the same ancient texts as the KJV but with updated language and grammar. I chose the NRSV for this text not because it sells the most but because it receives a broad endorsement from both denominations and scholars.

Chapter 3

Truth and truth in the Bible

Defining Myth

We are almost ready to look at the biblical texts themselves, beginning with the creation story in Genesis. It is not the purpose of this book to enter into the scientific and historical debates centered on the first few pages of the Bible. Perhaps, however, we can accomplish something even more useful by discovering common ground between those who might otherwise disagree about such matters.

To begin, let's consider a relatively safe example from the traditions of the ancient Greeks. When we read the words of the ancient Greek author Hesiod about Prometheus stealing fire or about Pandora letting human evil fly out of a box, we do not to ask whether these events actually occurred or could have occurred but whether they ring true in terms of the way humans act. In the case of Prometheus, we consider how people strive to come up with new, more powerful technologies and then pay a price; in the case of Pandora, we recognize how our curiosity sometimes gets us into trouble. Don't these insights represent the true value of these stories? Therefore, to call such stories *myths* is not to imply that the stories are false in terms of history or science but to imply that they are in fact true in terms of the human condition. A *myth*, by definition, is a primal story that conveys fundamental insights about reality. Pay close attention to that definition. Note that it contains the word "story" and the word "reality" without contradiction. While we might be interested to know if events in the story actually happened in history, that's not the point of the story or the point of myth. The point is the reality. Another way of putting this is that myth affirms Truth with a capital "T" (fundamental insights) whether or not it conveys truth with a small "t" (historical or scientific accuracy).

All human cultures have myths. A primal story is *primal* in the sense that it tells of the first events that formed the world and its people, and it is a *story* in the sense that it occurs as a narrative with a setting and characters, not merely a list of statements. That which is primal is not only first in chronological order but also basic and unchanging: what is true about life now and has always been true. Knowing what is primal provides life with order and stability. It is important for this to occur in a story in order to connect it with the ongoing story of humanity and with the story of each of us as individuals. We are hard-wired to seek such a connection with others, not only in the present but also in the past and future.

So it is a mistake to say of this or that text, "it is a myth and therefore not true," because the very nature of myth is to affirm Truth. But this may not be reassuring to those who look to the Bible as a guide to belief. They may believe that the Bible must contain both Truth with a big "T" (fundamental insight) and truth with a small "t" (historical or scientific accuracy) in order to be inspired and trustworthy on matters of faith. The presence of myth in the Bible may compromise its unique stature and make it just another artifact of ancient history. Then there is the "slippery slope" problem: if the creation story is not taken literally, then maybe other details are suspect, even the words and deeds of Jesus. Some of these concerns may be addressed, at least indirectly, in later parts of this book, as we consider kinds of writing in the Bible that differ in the way they are intended to be read. But for now, a modern story may offer a helpful perspective to both believers and nonbelievers.

Two Men and a Stormy Night

Before they became the two best-selling authors of the twentieth century, J. R. R. Tolkien and C. S. Lewis were young English professors at Oxford. Tolkien was a devout Roman Catholic and Lewis an atheist. Late one September evening in 1931, the two friends walked along a path for several hours discussing, of all things, the nature of myth.

For Lewis, the biblical story was important to the history of ideas, like similar stories in other cultures. He and Tolkien were classically educated in the Greek and Roman mythologies, and they shared a particular fascination for the northern European myths. But for Lewis, all such tales, including the biblical stories, were myths; and as he put it, "myths are lies, though lies breathed in silver."

Tolkien countered that God is behind even the pagan stories, expressing truth through the minds of poets, using images that were familiar in those cultures. Or to express this from the human perspective, myth is invention, but invention about truth. While the myths woven by humans contain error, Tolkien explained, they also contain a splintered fragment of the true light, the eternal truth that is with God. Our myths may be misguided, but they steer, however shakily, toward the true harbor. The difference in the case of the biblical account is that events actually occurred in history. Naturally, the myth of God enacted in history would be similar in some respects to other myths; this is simply how myth works.

Tolkien's explanation struck Lewis as an entirely new insight. He suggested to Tolkien that if this is true, the feelings of longing awakened by reading the pagan myths might be a kind of preparation for the Truth revealed in the biblical myth. Writing about this moment in their exchange a few days later, Lewis noted that just then, a great rush of wind blew the trees and sent a shower of leaves down upon them, as if (it seemed to them at the time) to confirm their words. Tolkien at this point urged Lewis to become a Christian. Within days, Lewis did just that—and the rest, as they say, is history. Lewis soon became arguably the most important Christian writer of the 20th century. Tolkien went on to write *The Lord of the Rings*, which he intended as a myth for England to serve as the Greco-Roman or Norse myths did for their cultures: to prepare readers to accept the Truth of Christianity.

The relevance of this story for our study of the Bible as literature is multifold. Tolkien and Lewis were prominent literary scholars who understood the distinction between truth and Truth in myth. Their understanding of the relation between biblical myths and other myths is also instructive. For the believer, it offers a way to understand the biblical account in relation to stories with similar features. For the nonbeliever, it suggests that there may be development in and connection between myths, and that myths may contain historical elements.

The Good Samaritan: true or True?

Because this distinction between truth and Truth can be particularly challenging to people of faith, I will offer one more illustration from the Bible itself. This example has proven helpful to a number of students who have approached me with concerns about their faith being compromised by challenges to the Bible's historical accuracy.

I would ask the student, first, to recall the story of the Good Samaritan in the Gospel of Luke, chapter 10. The student usually knows the story, told by Jesus, about a traveler who is attacked by thieves on the road, neglected by religious types, but helped by a "lowly" Samaritan. The lesson, of course, is to act like the Samaritan.

I then ask the student to tell me if the passage is a parable or an account of events that actually occurred. This is a stumper, because in fact the Gospel doesn't tell us.

My next question is, "Do you think it matters to Jesus whether we think of it as a parable or a story, as long as we act like the Samaritan?"

"No, of course not," the student inevitably responds.

"But still, we're curious," I continue, "so is there a method to tell us if the passage is history or parable?"

The more sophisticated student is aware of such a method, which is to compare the biblical passage to others like it, to see if it contains elements of parables or of historical accounts. (In this case, incidentally, the signs point to parable rather than historical account.) To apply such a method is to study the Bible as *literature*. This does not diminish the big "T" Truth, and such small "t" study may in fact contribute to spiritual insight. In any case, there is no need to feel threatened by the distinction. This method of study is simply a matter of honoring the rich diversity within the Bible, which includes poetic, mythic, parabolic, preachy, historical, and other kinds of writing. Sometimes an honest assessment comes down on the side of historical accounting, sometimes not; but for the believer, the biblical text always comes down on the side of Truth.

When truth and Truth Meet

It would be simplistic, however, to suggest that such assessment is never controversial, or that small "t" truth concerns are entirely independent of personal faith. At some point modern historical or scientific considerations meet the supernatural element in the Bible, acceptance of which is a matter of faith. That is, at some point small "t" and big "T" truth must either converge or diverge, whether in events like God's call of Abraham to be the first Jew, the Exodus of the Jews from Egypt, or the miracles and

Approaching the Bible as Literature

resurrection of Jesus. Orthodox faith affirms that these events occurred in history, not only in stories. Now, to be fair, one might adopt an *un*orthodox faith, regarding all of these events as non-historical but maintaining faith in God moment-by-moment: "existential" belief. Most people however, demand a faith with more substantial connections to real events.

My own recommendation to students of the Bible, whatever their faith commitments, is to resist notions about what one *must* believe or what one *cannot* believe and focus instead on what the biblical text says about itself. That is, if a passage or book shows clear signs of being written as history, then the writer expects us to regard the events described as historical—with allowance for variations in standards and styles between ancient and modern writers. If, however, the text shows signs that it is a kind of writing other than historical—parable, allegory, poetry, etc.—then the focus should be on the big "T" Truth element, not on small "t" truth issues like history.

In summary, since this text focuses on the Bible as *literature,* not the Bible as *true or false,* we will leave the ultimate questions open and consider instead the kind of writing we encounter in the Bible. In this way, those who come to the text with only an academic interest will grow in understanding, while those who come with a faith commitment will deepen their appreciation of God's artistry.

Section Two

Story and Meaning in Historical Narratives

Chapter 4

The Past Reveals the Present in Genesis 1–11

Now that we have considered important preliminaries about how the Bible came to us and how this textbook will approach it, we are ready to encounter the biblical text itself and invite the reader's own study and insight. We begin, naturally, "in the beginning" with the first chapters of Genesis. In order to focus on the literary and thematic aspects of this familiar text, I will ask you to set aside questions of science, history, and even theology in order to consider the book of Genesis in new ways. Read the questions on the next couple of pages, then read the text with the questions in mind. After responding to these questions, you will read several other creation stories and respond to further questions. The questions about Genesis and comparison to other creation accounts are designed to help you think about the *intentions* of the biblical text. If you are working in a group or class, comparison with others' responses will serve as the basis for discussion.

Read Genesis 1–3

4a: Think of the familiar story of creation and humanity's fall not as an account of beginnings but as a description of *the way things are* in terms of human nature, human relations, the natural world, and the nature of God. List five statements derived from the story that might be considered ongoing realities. Examples: "God brings order from chaos," or "Humanity has responsibility for nature."

4b: Explain what you think it means for humans to be "in the image of God" (1:26–27).

4c: Consider the story as the beginning of morality. What details, including symbols, reveal what is fundamentally good or bad? Compose a list of five statements. Example: "Order is better than chaos."

Read Creation Accounts From Other Cultures

Read the following creation stories from ancient India, North America, and Greece. The response questions will focus on similarities and differences that will help us to understand the Genesis account more deeply.

Hindu Creation Stories

Then nothingness was not, nor existence. There was no air then, nor the heavens beyond it. What covered it? Where was it? In whose keeping? Was there then cosmic water, in depths unfathomed? Then there were neither death nor immortality, nor was there then the torch of night and day. The One breathed windlessly and self-sustaining. There was that One then, and there was no other. At first there was only darkness wrapped in darkness. All this was only unilumined water. That One which came to be, enclosed in nothing, arose at last, born of the power of heat. In the beginning desire descended on it—that was the primal seed, born of the mind. The sages who have searched their hearts with wisdom know that which is, is kin to that which is not. And they have stretched their cord across the void, and know what was above, and what below. Seminal powers made fertile mighty forces. Below was strength, and over it was impulse. But, after all, who knows, and who can say whence it all came, and how creation happened? The gods themselves are later than creation, so who knows truly whence it has arisen? Whence all creation had its origin, he, whether he fashioned it or whether he did not, he, who surveys it all from highest heaven, he knows—or maybe even he does not know.

In the beginning, this universe was Soul in the form of the Man. He looked around and saw nothing other than himself.... He desired a second. He was of the same size and kind as a man and a woman closely embracing. He caused himself to fall into two pieces, and from him a husband and a wife were born.... He united with her, and from this mankind was born.

She reflected, "How can he unite with me after engendering me from himself? For shame! I will conceal myself." She became a cow; he became a bull and united with her, and from this all cattle were born. She became a mare; he became a stallion. She became a female ass, he a male ass and united with her, and from this all whole-hooved animals were born.... Thus he created all pairs, even down to the ants. He knew that he was creation, for he created all of this. Thus creation arose.

North American (Inuit) Creation Story

In the beginning there was only darkness. Yet, in that darkness, there was already Raven. He was still small and weak and his special powers had not fully developed. In fact, he did not even know that he had special powers. He crouched in the ground in the darkness, listening. There was no sound. Nothing. He felt around him. The ground was hard and bare. Cautiously at first, then with growing confidence, he crawled forward over the ground. Everywhere it seemed the same—hard and bare. But behind him, as he moved, things began to come to life. Water trickled out of crevices, swelling to become streams and rivers. Hills and mountains pushed up out of the earth. By the time that Raven returned to the place where he had started, he was astonished to find a forest with a thick undergrowth of grass and ferns.

Encouraged by this, he decided to explore further but, before he had gone very far, he stopped and drew back in alarm. The ground had disappeared! He was on the edge of a yawning crevasse and only empty space lay before him. He rested under a tree and tried to puzzle it all out. Who was he? What made things grow? What lay at the bottom of the crevasse? Perched on the edge of the chasm, he flexed his wings and felt them grow strong and powerful. All at once everything became clear. He knew who he was! He was Tuluaukuk, the Raven Father, the creator of all life. With a triumphant, "Cawk! Cawk!," he spread his wings and glided down into the silent and mysterious darkness.

Far below, he found another land, so new that the crust had barely begun to harden. Raven called this land "earth" and the land which he had left behind he called "sky." Earth was barren and desolate, just as the Sky Land had been, but by his very presence Raven brought it to life and soon this land, too, was covered with trees, grass, plants, and flowers.

Yet, all the while, darkness covered everything. Suddenly a pin-point of light caught his eye. Bending down, he glimpsed a fragment of mica half-hidden in the ground. As he scraped away the soil, the light grew brighter—much, much brighter. Shielding his eyes from the glare, Raven tossed the mica high in the air and in an instant the world was flooded with brilliant sunshine.

Now Raven could see what he had created. It was a wonderful land of high, snow-capped mountains, forests and wooded slopes, of grassy plains and valleys, well watered with rivers, lakes, and streams, bright and shining in the clear light. Raven walked about the beautiful new land, proudly surveying his handiwork. On the seashore a giant beach-pea vine caught his eye. It was much larger than the others, tall as a birch tree and heavy with pale green pods.

Suddenly, with a loud pop, one of the pods burst open and out tumbled a man! Startled by this unexpected apparition, Raven jumped back. The first Eskimo sat on the ground, rubbing his eyes in the bright light. "Well!" cried Raven. "When I made the beach-pea, I never thought that something like this would come out of it!"

When they had both recovered from their surprise, Raven showed Man what he had done. "Are you hungry?" asked Raven. "These berries are good to eat." Man ate the berries, but he still felt hungry and Raven saw that something more sustaining was required. After a little thought, he took a lump of clay from the river bank and fashioned two little animals with short sturdy legs and broad, curving horns. He lowered his wings over them for a moment and, when he raised them again, two great musk-oxen bounded away over the plain.

For several days Raven went about making all kinds of animals, birds and fish, and explaining their uses to man. Thinking that Man might be lonely by himself, Raven decided to give him a companion. He made a little clay figure, rather like Man in appearance, with a knot of fine grass for hair. Raven flapped his wings--and there stood the first woman!

Greek Creation Stories

First of all, Chaos came into existence; afterwards came broad-bosomed Earth, the everlasting seat of all the deathless gods who inhabit the heights of Olympus. Then came murky Tartarus [the underworld], tucked into the depth of the earth; also Eros, most beautiful god among all the immortals, who loosens limbs and dominates hearts and the minds and disrupts well-laid plans of both gods and men. Next, Chaos coupled with Erebus [hell] to give birth to black Night; then, after conceiving with Erebus, Chaos gave birth to Aether [the upper air] and Daylight together. Earth gave birth first to star-studded Heaven [sky], equal in size to herself, to conceal her on every side, in order to furnish a place for the gods to dwell forever. Next Earth gave birth to enormous mountains, the pleasant retreats of goddesses. [The text lists several more gods born from Earth.] Heaven and Earth bore, last of their children, intelligent Cronus, their strongest and boldest offspring, who hated his lusty father. [From this point, the gods start fighting, sometimes creating other gods out of the torn-up bits of others. Eventually, Zeus and the other more familiar gods are created, along with immortals called Titans, including Prometheus (=forethought) and Epimetheus (=afterthought), whose task was to populate the earth with men. There were no women yet. We pick up the story in another text:]

Therefore almighty Zeus plotted sorrows and troubles for mankind. He hid fire, which Prometheus, Iapetus's great-hearted son, stole from Zeus to benefit mankind and hid in a hollowed-out stalk to baffle the lover of thunder. Then cloud-gathering Zeus said in anger to Prometheus: "Iapetus's brat, since you're so much smarter than anyone else, and happy to outwit me, and rejoice in the fire you have stolen—for yourself and for the men of the future I will provide a calamity. For I shall give them something terrible in exchange for this fire which they all find so wonderful." Then the father of gods and of mankind burst into laughter. He commanded Hephaestus, the world-famed craftsman, to mix water and earth, give it human speech and strength, and to make it look like a goddess, with a pretty and lovable feminine form. He made Athena instruct her in domestic skills, and he made gold Aphrodite drip charm over her head to cause men to long for her and exhaust their bodies in anguish over her. Finally, Zeus gave instructions to Hermes, the sure guide, slayer of Argus, to put in her the heart of a bitch and a devious nature. . . . He called her Pandora [many gifts], because all who inhabit lofty Olympus had given something to pretty Pandora, the great bane to industrious mankind.

When he had finished this downright desperate piece of deception, Zeus sent to Epimetheus the famous swift messenger of the immortals, Hermes, with Pandora as a present. Epimetheus had forgotten Prometheus's warning not to accept anything from Olympian Zeus but to send it back where it came from lest it become a disaster for mortals. [Along with Pandora, Zeus sent to Epimetheus a wedding gift, a jar filled with evils, knowing that the woman would not be able to resist opening the jar to find out what was inside.]

Until that time, all the various tribes of the human race dwelt on earth on their own and remote from evils, difficult labor, and distressing diseases that bring doom closer to each one. Now, using her fingers, the maid [Pandora] pried open the lid of the great jar, sprinkling out its contents; and so she brought sad hardships to mankind. Only Hope stayed under the rim of the jar and did not fly away, for in compliance with the wishes of cloud-gathering Zeus, Pandora put the lid back on the jar before Hope could come out. The rest of the contents wander among men as numberless sorrows, since earth and sea teem with miseries.

4d: What are three features that most or all of the creation accounts, including Genesis, have in common?

4e: How does the character of the creator(s) in each of these accounts differ from the character of the creator in Genesis?

4f: How does the Genesis account differ from the others in terms of historical realism?

Read Genesis 4–11

4g: The flood story is one of the stories in the Bible that most appeals to children. Apart from the simplistic "everyone loves animals," what are reasons for this?

4h: The flood account, especially the aftermath, can be viewed as a new creation story. How does the beginning of Chapter 9 constitute a more "advanced" form of the original arrangements with humans in 1:28 and 3:16–24?

Acknowledgments:

The Hindu creation accounts are from the *Rig Veda* (2000–1700 BC) and the *Brhadaranyaka Upanishad* (550 BC), respectively. The translation is by Wendy Doniger Flaherty, *Hindu Myths*. Penguin: New York, 1975. Pp. 34–35.

The North American creation account: Wood, Marion. "The Coming of Raven." In *Spirits, Heroes, and Hunters from North American Indian Mythology*. New York: Peter Bedrick Books, 1992. Pp. 17–20.

The Greek creation account: from *Theogeny* lines 112–134 and *Works and Days*, lines 50–97, my own paraphrase based primarily on the translation of Daryl Hyne. *Works of Hesiod and the Homeric Hymns*. Chicago: University of Chicago Press, 2005. Pp. 25–26, 57–59.

For Further Study:

There are myriad additional questions presented by the story of creation in Genesis and by its comparison to other creation texts. Here are a few:

1. Scholars consider myth to be a justification of essential beliefs about humanity and society that give stability to ideas about the world. In what sense could a current scientific story of creation, like the Big Bang theory, be considered a myth?

2. What would be the implication if Gen 1:28 was translated to command humanity to "take responsibility for" rather than "have dominion over" the earth? What is the difference between a lord and a steward?

3. Does the Fall story imply that the attainment of moral knowledge is wrong or that obedience is more important than independent judgment?

4. Does the story of the first human pair (Gen 2:18–25) suggest that companionship, even marriage, is necessary to full humanness, or is the text merely attributing this universal compulsion to God's design?

5. Who is most responsible for the human condition of alienation and death according to the story of the Fall (Gen 3:14–24): God, humanity, or the serpent? To the extent that humanity is responsible, does the text lay more blame on Eve than Adam?

6. Do the similarities in creation stories suggest a common origin or universal human experience?

7. What are the implications of parallels between the biblical account and other creation stories produced in the ancient Near East? Comparisons have been made between the Genesis account and, for example, the *Epic of Gilgamesh*. This and other ancient creation accounts tend to be fragmentary and difficult to read without considerable help, which is why they are not included here. See the appendix on further reading for this chapter to find recommended texts.

Chapter 5

Telling the Story Well
Narrative Technique in Genesis and Exodus

Before continuing with the historical narratives beginning in Genesis 12, it is useful to explain a few terms and principles to guide our reading of ancient texts as literature, and to introduce themes to look for.

The stories of Abraham, Isaac, Jacob, and Joseph are known as the *patriarchal narratives* because these characters are regarded as the fathers of the nation. The initial key event is the call of Abram (later re-named Abraham), in which God promises to make a great nation of his descendants in the approximate location of modern Israel. This *Abrahamic Covenant*, which is repeated numerous times in the Bible, is the starting point for the people's ethnic and religious identity. In the Bible, the descendants of Abraham are called the Hebrews, Israelites, or children of Israel; the term "Jews" (after Judah, the fourth son of Jacob) begins after the sixth century BC, and by New Testament times it was the usual designation. Genesis (Greek: "beginnings"), combined with the next four books of the Bible, constitutes the historical foundation known as the Pentateuch or Torah. The approximate dates for the events of the patriarchal narratives are 2000–1800 BC. The time of Moses, including the Jewish Exodus (Greek for "journey") from Egypt, is traditionally dated about 1500–1400 BC.

Although every kind of biblical writing (law, prophecy, wisdom, poetry, romance) was also produced by other ancient Near Eastern cultures, there are very few ancient parallels to the colorful, detailed portrayals of individuals in the Bible such as those found in the historical books. It is remarkable that in an age of epic poetry, the Jews chose to tell their stories in narrative form; conversely, the substantial quantity of poetry in the Bible almost never involves storytelling. This extraordinary focus on *narrative* depiction of important characters may help to explain the more life-like, complex portraits of these individuals as compared to the idealistic, heroic depiction of characters in epic poetry. One of the most distinctive characteristics of the biblical stories, and one which extends from the patriarchs to later major characters like Moses, Saul, David, and Solomon, is that they are not idealized heroes but highly conflicted, sometimes contradictory characters. In other words, they are real; and it is this realism, not their saintly qualities, that accounts for their ongoing interest to readers despite the distance in time from their culture and even beliefs.

Approaching the Bible as Literature

Thousands of volumes have been devoted to the theological content of these books, their historical accuracy, and debates about when, how, and by whom they were written. We will touch on a few of these issues, but our focus is on the way the different kinds of writing work. Story or narrative is a particular genre of writing that uses certain elements to draw the reader in to the ideas the writer wants to convey. These ideas are sometimes quite complex and subtle. When this genre is most effective, the reader not only wants to know what happens next (the classic "page turner") but also wants to ponder or discuss the message. Scholars agree that the biblical narratives are masterful examples of the narrative genre.

The elements of effective narrative are probably familiar to you. But just as you enjoy a good meal without asking how it was prepared, so you enjoy a good story without critical analysis. You may even fear that such analysis might spoil your enjoyment—like stopping in the middle of that yummy meal, while the food cools, to interview the chef. You may find, however, that knowing in advance something about the recipe and the careful combination of ingredients can actually enhance your enjoyment of the meal.

Key Elements of Effective Narrative

1. Limitation of Explanation

Effective stories give just enough detail to make the characters and situations come to life but do not bog the reader down in religious or psychological commentary. This invites the reader to think and to reach independent insight.

2. Dominance of the Dramatic Approach

While simple direct reporting, detailed description of characters and scenes, and commentary on how the reader should react are all legitimate parts of narrative, the sense of encounter is best served by a story that includes dialogues and speeches by key characters. This technique allows the writer to "show" rather than "tell," to recreate an experience that readers can enter.

3. Use of Rhetorical Devices

Repetition is probably the most important technique used by biblical writers to aid memory and appreciation of key ideas. Repetition may involve words, phrases, images, actions, or ideas. There are many other rhetorical devicesperiod after "devices." *Simile* is a form of comparison in which one object "is like" another. *Metaphor* compares more strongly by saying that an object simply "is" or represents another. *Pattern,* such as groups of threes and *chiasm* (an X-shaped story where details lead to and then from a central event or idea) also help the reader to build up to, or discover within, the key ideas of a story. *Allusion* involves reference to an event, image, or even figure of speech used elsewhere in the Bible and is often hard to detect without extensive knowledge or help like a concordance (listing of words). *Foreshadowing* enriches a story by providing hints of what is to come. *Irony* suggests the opposite of literal meaning, or (dramatic irony) offers information known to the reader but not to the characters.

4. Use of Archetypes

There are certain universal symbols, character types, and story lines that we find endlessly repeated, even in our dreams. Finding them in a story gives us an old, familiar framework in which to discover new insights. While we will look at these in more detail as they apply to biblical poetry, a few are worth mentioning here because they are important in the patriarchal narratives: the quest, the death-rebirth motif, the initiation, the journey, the childless parents, tragedy (fall from innocence), and comedy (a happy ending, usually involving marriage and children). We will consider these in more detail in a subsequent chapter about poetry.

5. Effective Use of Setting

A good storyteller tells just enough of the physical (scenery), temporal (when events occurred), and cultural (customs) setting to make the story vivid in our imagination, to reinforce character and action, and to provide structural unity.

6. Creation of Plot Suspense

Effective storytelling makes readers want more by setting up tests, journeys, opponents, and dramatic irony. A sense that action is rising toward a turning point and resolution is satisfying to a reader.

7. Believable Characters

A character's words, personal traits and abilities, motivations, relationships, responses, and growth through events all signal a complex, flawed person with whom we can relate and from whom we might learn. It is easy to describe a successful character; only a handful of writers in history have successfully produced them.

This list is a lot to absorb, but it may be summarized in one phrase: appreciation of artistry. Some may argue that art does not mix well with lists and detailed explanations, just as appreciation of a flower may not be helped by dissection. If beauty is something that delights us and draws us in, should we risk being turned away by over-analysis? On the other hand, a person who takes a course in the history of art, or who learns how to paint, is likely to have a richer experience in a gallery. Conversely, a person who never attempts to understand the appeal of certain kinds of art is more apt to be swayed by what is merely trendy—a danger that is just as real in other realms, such as music, books, ideas, and of course religion.

It is crucial to understand, then, that this list of elements in effective storytelling is about art: the crafting of truth in a way that we might call beautiful. It may come as a surprise to learn that the Bible, a book supposedly about ultimate truths and issues of good vs. evil, conveys these ideas with the intention of beauty rather than in a straightforward list of propositions. If this book is inspired by God, the believer must conclude that God likes beauty at least as much as truth and goodness. If, on the other hand, this book is merely a human creation, its artistry helps to explain why it continues to attract and intrigue people over time.

Themes to Look for in the Patriarchal Narratives

To spell out all the ideas that one "ought" to discover in the patriarchal narratives would contradict the nature of these texts and the very notion inherent in these narratives, that one should discover truth through interaction with story. Before offering specific questions to encourage interaction with particular passages, I will suggest a series of questions to keep in mind while reading the patriarchal narratives. I will return to these questions later in the text.

1. What is the character of God as revealed in these stories? Is God predictable, fair, and merciful? Is God surprising in any way?

2. What qualities are demanded of successful characters? Are these the same qualities that you consider admirable today?

3. What role does opposition (internal conflict and external forces) play in the working out of God's purposes according to these stories?

4. Since even the first readers of these narratives lived long after the events described, what should the descendants of the patriarch—either in the ethnic or spiritual sense—understand about themselves as a result of these stories?

Telling the Story Well

Read Genesis 12–24

5a: Choose any three of the seven elements of effective storytelling outlined above and explain how each of the three applies in the narrative of Abraham, from his call to the sacrifice of Isaac.

Read Genesis 25–33

5b: Choose any two of the seven elements of effective storytelling that you did not use to answer the previous question and explain how each of the two applies in the narrative of Jacob and Esau.

Read Genesis 37–50

5c: How might events and character traits in the Joseph narrative be understood as representing the struggle of the Jewish people to build a national identity?

Read Exodus 1–20

5d: Both fire and water are important in the story of Moses and the Exodus. Give at least two examples of each from this section and explain what you think they symbolize.

For Further Study:

Questions 1–4 recall the questions introduced before you read the Genesis and Exodus narratives.

1. What is the character of God as revealed in these stories? Is God predictable, fair, merciful? Is God surprising in any way?
2. What qualities are demanded of successful characters? Are these the same qualities that most people consider admirable today?
3. What role does opposition (internal conflict and external forces) play in the working out of God's purposes according to these stories?
4. Since even the first readers of these narratives lived long after the events described, what should the descendants of the patriarch—either in the ethnic or spiritual sense—understand about themselves as a result of these stories?
5. Compare and contrast Abraham, Jacob, or Joseph to a familiar literary character representing the values of another culture, including our own. Possibilities include Odysseus, Pip in *Great Expectations*, Harry Potter, and Neo from *The Matrix*.
6. Of the seven elements of effective narrative described in this text, which would you argue is most important in securing the lasting impact of the patriarchal narratives?

Chapter 6

Narrative from Exodus to Samuel

Summary of Early Historical Books

The enormous size of the Bible requires that, at this introductory level, we must pass over large portions, including important parts of the history of Israel, which I will summarize along with a general description of the books we are not reading. These early sections of the Bible include an important category of biblical writing, the law code, that we will mention here only in passing. While lists of required and prohibited behaviors, including detailed descriptions of religious buildings and rituals, may not engage the beginning student, it is important to note that such material has an important history, a distinctive literary style, and a far-reaching impact in terms of the development of religion and morality.

After chapter 20, the book of *Exodus* (Greek: "journey") goes into detail about moral and ceremonial laws, festivals, and the *tabernacle:* a temporary, traveling temple which served as the Israelite's center of worship during their wanderings.

The book of *Leviticus* (Greek: "relating to the Levites [priests]") is a kind of manual for the Israelite priests and contains many laws governing morality and ritual purity. It also describes in detail what is to this day the most important Jewish holiday, the Day of Atonement (Yom Kippur).

The book of *Numbers,* so named because of it contains several census name lists, also describes much drama during Israel's forty years in the Sinai wilderness, ending with the people poised to invade Canaan (roughly, the southern two-thirds of modern Israel). Their constant grumbling, indicating a lack of faith, is the cause for this delay of entry to the Promised Land.

Deuteronomy (Greek: "second law") is a kind of reinterpretation of the first four books of the Bible, portraying Moses as a preacher who explains the law as God's covenant with his people, with promises for obedience and sanctions for neglect. In terms of Judaism and its focus on following God's will as revealed in the law, Deuteronomy is regarded by many as the most important book in the Old Testament.

Joshua tells the story of the conquest of Canaan. The main character, named by Moses as his successor, does a lot of "smiting" in a holy war that sometimes involves annihilating cities with all their inhabitants. By the end of the book, the Israelites have apportioned their new territory according to tribes (named for the twelve sons of Jacob/Israel) and are well established in the central hill country.

Judges describes a sad chapter in Israel's early history, characterized by worship of idols rather than God, military setbacks in the struggle with the Canaanites for dominance of the area, and, finally, civil war. These judges, the most famous of which was Samson, were military leaders who sometimes served to unify the people, but the complaint of the biblical writers is that during this period "all the people did what was right in their own eyes" (21:25).

Ruth, just five pages long, is set in the period of judges, before Israel had a king. It is a remarkable story from a literary standpoint, delivering a message of loyalty to God and family with rich characterization, romance, and high drama. Indeed, although the story is insignificant in terms of Israel's history and religion, it is a prime biblical example of masterful storytelling, reinforcing core themes by inviting the reader to ponder the meaning of the narrative.

The Books of Samuel and Kings

1–2 Samuel and *1–2 Kings* tell the story of Israel's rocky road to monarchy. After a "golden age" under David and Solomon, the realm was divided into two kingdoms and ultimately conquered by the empires on its borders. David is a central figure in the history of Israel and a worthwhile focus of our literary study because he is masterfully crafted as a character. In some ways he provides a heroic contrast to the tragic figure of his predecessor, Saul; in other ways David himself is tragic, his flaws of ambition and desire coming back to haunt him and his nation's history.

1 Samuel begins with the story of Samuel, who serves as both judge (military leader) and prophet (spokesman for God). He hopes to encourage the people of Israel to devote themselves to God, but they have a different idea. They want a king, believing that the consolidation of power around one person will give them status to compete with the surrounding nations. God grudgingly grants their request, and Samuel *anoints* (pours symbolic oil upon) Saul, who is designated for the office. Unfortunately, Saul disobeys God's will regarding the nature of his military operations, and he is told that his reign will be short-lived. We pick up the action with God's new choice for king.

Read 1 Samuel 16–17

6a: What indications of David's character, both good and bad, are given in this story that may set up events to come?

Read 1 Samuel 18–31

6b: The point of this section is to contrast two men, one on the way up and one on the way down. But both characters remain a complicated mix of good and bad traits. What does the storyteller do to make the tragic figure Saul more sympathetic, and what does he do to show the heroic figure David as less than perfect?

Approaching the Bible as Literature

Read 2 Samuel 1–12

6c: How does the narrator use dramatic irony to heighten the effect of Nathan's confrontation of David?

Read 2 Samuel 13–18

6d: How does the Absalom episode show the conflict between David's political life and his personal life?

The Rest of the Story

The remaining chapters of 1 Samuel take David into a sad old age. Beginning with the book of 1 Kings, following David's death, his son Solomon rises to prominence, consolidates David's military successes, and constructs the temple, which will be the center of Israelite worship for several hundred years. But Solomon, like his father, becomes a victim of his own desires, taking on many wives and building structures to honor his wives' gods. The nation suffers a civil war, and soon after Solomon's death, the nation splits into northern and southern kingdoms, Israel and Judah. The rest of 1–2 Kings (1–2 Chronicles covers the same period with somewhat different emphases) tells the up-and-down story of various Israelite kings, some of whom obey God, others who neglect God and worship idols. The northern kingdom of Israel is conquered by the Assyrian empire (centered in modern-day Syria) in 722 BC, and the southern kingdom holds out until a new power, Babylon (centered in modern-day Iraq), conquers Judah in 587 BC. The Babylonians destroy the temple and send many of the ruling class of Jews into exile. The short book of Esther tells of a Jewish heroine during the time of the exile. Ezra and Nehemiah chronicle the Jews' return from exile under the new Persian Empire, when they rebuild the temple, fortify Jerusalem, and experience a religious revival. This completes the historical books of the Old Testament, although much of Israel's history is conveyed indirectly in the prophetic writings and even in the Book of Psalms, which we will consider next.

For Further Study:

1. Compare Moses or David to a familiar historical character from our era such as Abraham Lincoln, Mahatma Gandhi, or Martin Luther King Jr. Can you find elements of the biblical narrative that served as direct or indirect inspiration for the activities of these figures?

2. For a fuller picture of Saul, add 1 Sam 8–15 to the story and comment on the features of effective narrative that contribute to his portrayal as a tragic figure.

3. Read the following passages and discuss whether the Old Testament might be used today to justify "holy war" and genocide: Exod 15:1–3, Josh 6–8, 11: 12–14, 22:8; Deut 5:17, 20:1–20, 23:9–14, 2 Kings 3:4. Are there other biblical principles that come into play to construct a position on the morality of war?

4. Read 1 Kings 1–11 and comment on the narrative features that convey the positive and negative aspects of the career of Solomon.

5. In the midst of the long chronicle of alternating good and bad kings occurs the story of a prophet, Elijah the Tishbite (1 Kings 17–2 Kings 2). What features of this story may contribute to the later expectation for Jews and Christians (based on Malachi 3:19) that Elijah would return in some sense to precede the messiah?

6. Considering as many major biblical figures as possible, would you characterize them as heroic role models, moral examples, or complex characters impossible to classify? How has your study of them modified your view of how biblical narrative works?

Chapter 7

From Solomon to the Close of the Old Testament

The purpose of placing historical material here is twofold: to fill out the history of Israel for the narrative sections of the Old Testament that we will *not* read, and to put in context the other kinds of Old Testament writing that we will read in later sections of this text.

The Land of the People

It is remarkable that most biblical history is packed into an area approximately the size and shape of New Hampshire. From Dan to Beersheba, the towns marking the traditional north-sound frontiers of Israel, is a mere 144 miles, and from the Mediterranean Sea to the Jordan River is about 75 miles. For most of Israel's ancient history, the bulk of the population lived in less than half of that area.

It is useful to visualize the terrain as three strips running north to south. The most fertile area is the western coastal plain along the Mediterranean Sea, which for much of the biblical period was occupied not by Israelites but by Canaanites or Philistines. The Israelites were concentrated in the central hill country, which includes Jerusalem in the south. This area rises to 3000 feet in elevation and receives a fair amount of rain but is generally arid. The eastern third of the land is mostly desert and sparsely inhabited. Two inland bodies of water, the Sea of Galilee and the Dead Sea, are joined by the Jordan River. The surface of the Sea of Galilee is 600 feet below sea level, and the area around it is fertile and prosperous. The Dead Sea is 1200 feet below sea level, and the surrounding area is an inhospitable wasteland of sun-baked rock.

Why did such a small land, much of it sparsely inhabited, become so pivotal in human history? While the focus of the story rightly falls on the people involved, geography plays a part as well. For thousands of years, Palestine's roads were the only viable trade routes between Egypt and the great civilizations to the north and east. Indeed, because the area effectively links three continents—Asia, Africa, and Europe—the march of human history must pass this way, quite literally. The biblical narrative comes into focus when one man, Abraham, wanders into this place of promise in response to the call of his God. From Abraham's tent ultimately arose the city of Jerusalem, home to three major religions that today encompass half the world's population. The Jews themselves, though exiled from their homeland for long periods, have exerted an enormous influence on history even while in exile. But for the faithful, the land—the *Promised* Land of their sacred texts—never loses its significance.

Establishment in Palestine

Abraham and his first descendants lived in Palestine from 1800–1600 BC. According to the biblical account, they thrived until famine drove them to the more fertile Egypt, where they settled and were used by the pharaohs as cheap or slave labor. Egypt, the dominant power in the area, was sparsely populated except for the Nile River valley, and the Egyptians maintained military and commercial outposts along the Mediterranean coast. So when the Israelites under Moses left in the Exodus, they travelled inland through the Sinai desert and eventually crossed into Palestine from the east, across the Jordan River. There is much dispute among scholars about precisely when and how this invasion took place, but the Israelites eventually consolidated power under kings David and Solomon between 1000–900 BC. This hardly qualified as an empire, but the Jews did dominate the region for a time, partly because the larger realms of Egypt to the south and Assyria to the north were in decline.

Conquest to Return from Exile

Soon after Solomon's death, civil unrest caused a split into a northern kingdom called Israel, with its capital in the city of Samaria, and a southern kingdom called Judah, with its capital in Jerusalem. Rivalries and infighting characterized the next two hundred years, and the biblical narrative describes a gradual decline under kings who increasingly turned away from God. Eventually Assyria, a new empire to the north and east, rose to prominence in the region and in 722 BC conquered Israel.

Judah continued for some time as a small kingdom under the shadow of Assyria, but its days were numbered. At one point, the emperor Sennacharib besieged Jerusalem under king Hezekiah and withdrew—a rare example of an event recorded both by Jewish and Assyrian sources. But out of the frying pan, into the fire: the Babylonian empire succeeded the Assyrians and conquered Judah in 587 BC. The Babylonians destroyed the first Jewish temple, which had been built by Solomon, and surviving Jewish leaders were sent into exile. Some of them became established in Babylon and did not return even when allowed decades later. Thus began the Jewish *diaspora* (Greek for "dispersion"), which established Jewish settlements all over the ancient world. By the New Testament era, such settlements were spread throughout the Roman Empire and Jews numbered about 7 percent of its population.

The Persian Empire succeeded the Babylonian in the sixth century BC. One of its first emperors, Cyrus, allowed religious freedom in exchange for tribute, a revolutionary approach that helped the Persians to build the largest empire in world history up to that time, stretching from near India to the Mediterranean. Under one of Cyrus's successors, Darius, the exiled Jews were allowed to return to their homeland. Beginning about 450 BC under the leadership of Ezra and Nehemiah, these returning Jews rebuilt Jerusalem's walls, reconstructed the temple, and led a religious reform focused on renunciation of idolatry (worship of gods other than Jahweh) and obedience to the religious law.

We will resume the history of Israel in Section Four, where the focus is on events and ideas that set the stage for the New Testament.

Approaching the Bible as Literature

For Further Study:

1. Research an issue of historical debate like the date of the Exodus, the archaeology of the conquest, or the kingdoms of David and Solomon and comment on the truth/Truth distinction described earlier in this text.

2. As citizens of a dominant world power, modern Americans find it difficult to view history and current events from the point of view of an underdog. How do major events (exodus, exile and return, struggles for independence) in Israel's history during the biblical period affect the writers' perspectives on the present and future? [This question may be answered more thoroughly after a consideration of prophetic literature and the psalms.]

3. How do the stories of Abraham, Joseph, Moses, and David show the character of the nation Israel? What four stories, and for what four characters, would you choose to show the character of America? How is the spiritual element more or less important in either list?

Section Three

Poetry, Problems, and Promise in Psalms, Prophecy, and Wisdom

Chapter 8

Principles of Hebrew Poetry

One third of the Bible is poetry. This should hardly surprise us: in all times and cultures, people have turned to song to express their deepest human yearnings for inner peace, justice, and understanding. And interestingly, we turn most often to poetry not when we are happy but when we want to express pain, alienation, and longing. Biblical poetry reflects this tendency to address problems more than to celebrate solutions. The Book of Psalms, sometimes called the songbook of the Bible, is the obvious place to begin our study. But nineteen other Old Testament books are entirely or mostly poetry, and there is at least one poetic passage in sixteen other Old Testament books. Only the get-down-to-business law code Leviticus and the brief narrative books Nehemiah and Esther are without poetry. In the New Testament, eighteen books contain at least a bit of poetry; the exceptions are short letters. From the first words spoken by a human (Gen 2:23) to the announcement of the end of time (Rev 21:1–4), the Bible hums with song.

And yet how does one sing along? Although modern translators put much of the Bible in stanzas to indicate poetic form, we do not see elements of poetry familiar to us like rhyme and meter. This is primarily because ancient poetry operates by a different set of rules; but as we will see, some of these are familiar.

To explain the technique of the ancient Hebrew writers, however, does not tell us why they chose poetry. Part of the explanation is that words written in patterned form are easier to remember, and that made poetry useful before writing was widespread. Furthermore, humanity's deepest yearnings and highest thoughts have always involved language that reaches beyond rational propositions, and poetry (often set to music) serves the whole person, not just the mind.

But there is more. We will observe a distinctive element in Hebrew poetry that sometimes escapes notice because it has so influenced our view of the world that we tend to take it for granted. This dominant feature of Hebrew poetry is its movement through crisis toward resolution, a resolution that in these writings is provided by God, whose power works for the benefit of the individual or the nation. Note three key elements here: a linear view of time (as compared, for example, to a cyclical model in Asian thought), fundamental optimism (as opposed to modern Western despair), and resolution "from above" (as opposed to human solutions). As we will see, these elements are written into the very rulebook of Hebrew poetry.

Why are these elements important? We might ask why people love to climb hills and mountains. A path uphill carries with it the anticipation of culmination. Drama mounts as the way becomes steeper, as we recognize our own weakness, as we wonder if and when we will arrive, and then we experience the release and relief of the summit. This, in biblical terms, is the vision and journey of redemption, which is built into the very structure of Hebrew verse.

Poetry of this kind is a medium of hope. What is fascinating is that the poetic method has such an influence on the message. Just as the tonal qualities of certain instruments affect the kind of music we produce, or as certain kinds of stone affect the production of sculpture, so also the techniques available to the Hebrew poets produced—or at least strengthened—a particular set of ideas.

Ancient and Modern Poetry

After reading several Hebrew poems, *déjà vu* begins to set in: you notice similar lines and the same images, sometimes in the same poem. By contrast, modern English poetry tries to grab your attention with surprising images and unusual combinations of words. This is in part a cultural difference. In our fast-paced world, we are bored by the familiar and demand novelty. In the biblical world, however, higher value was placed on repetition and a limited number of images, perhaps combined in new ways, in order to encourage the audience to pause and ponder. To appreciate the difference, think about what you see from your car while driving as compared to what you see along the same road during a long walk. In the biblical world, everybody walked. So let us slow down with them and take in the view.

Hebrew Poetry Techniques Lost in Translation

Some sophisticated techniques of Hebrew poetry are largely lost when translated into English. But even at this introductory level, it is worth briefly describing just a few of these to give you a sense of the many literary gems hidden just beneath the surface of translation.

Meter is the rhythm of accented syllables. English poetry until the late nineteenth century—and of course today's music lyrics—is written in meter, most often in four- or five-beat lines. Familiar examples may be found in the classic iambic pentameter of Shakespeare, Milton, and Frost, with ten syllables and a stress on the second, fourth, etc.: "Shall I compare thee to a summer's day?" Hebrew poetry usually employs three-beat lines (less commonly, two or four), which is why the lines are usually short in English translation. Note the accented syllables in this pair of three-beat lines from 2 Samuel 22:30: "For with *you* I *charge* a *bar*rier / with my *God* I *vault* a *wall*." Now try to pronounce the words in transliterated Hebrew: *Ki békha arúts gedúd / be lohái adáleg shúr.*

Alliteration is the repetition of consonants in words grouped closely together, usually at the beginning of words. We use this technique sparingly for effect in modern English, e.g., "pick your poison" or "flags of our fathers," or the classic tongue-twister, "Peter Piper picked a peck of pickled peppers." A simple example from the Bible is Isa 1:18: "Though your sins are like scarlet (*kashinim*), they shall be like snow (*kasheleg*). Ps 46:9 repeats the staccato sounds *q* and *t* to convey the shattering sounds of conflict: "He makes the wars cease to the ends of the earth (*masbit milchamot 'ad-qesheh ha'ares*), he breaks the bow, and shatters the spear" (*qeset yesaber weqisses hanit*).

Assonance is the repetition of vowels in words grouped closely together. This is a techniques that we use less often in English: "How now brown cow?" An example from Hebrew poetry is Prov 11:2: "When pride comes, then comes disgrace" (*bah zadón wayávo kalón*). Note that there is even an internal rhyme here, *zadón* and *kalón*. Both alliteration and assonance occur in Isa 29:2, "heaviness and sorrow" (*ta' aniya wa' aniya*).

Paronomasia (Greek: "near sound") is pun. After brooding on the fowl housing market, I hatched an idea for a hen house in the shape of a vintage car, which I call a chicken *coupe*. The Hebrew prophets loved such word play. In Amos 8:1, the prophet is shown a "basket of summer fruit" (*qayits*) to signify the "end" (*qets*) of Israel. Psalm 5:9 likens the heart (*qerbam*) of one who brings destruction to an open sepulcher (*qeber*). Jeremiah 1:11–12 has the prophet shown an almond branch (*shaqed*) to signify that God is watching (*shoqed*) over his word.

Acrostic is a technique in which the first letters of parts of the poem follow the sequence of the alphabet. The most famous biblical example is the longest psalm, 119, each stanza of which begins with one of the twenty-four letters of the Hebrew alphabet. The scheme is used in eight other psalms (9, 10, 24, 24, 37, 111, 112, 145), Prov 31:10–31, Lamentations 1–4, and Nahum 1.

Onomatopoeia is the use of words that sound like the action they describe. Common English examples include body noises like "burp," "cough," and "spit." Psalm 140:3 uses "s" sounds for "They make their tongue sharp as a serpent's: *šanenu lesonam kemo-nahas*. Isaiah 5:30 predicts that Israel's enemies "will roar over it on that day like the roaring of the sea." Try to pronounce the Hebrew original, and listen for the sea in the big, hollow vowels: *weyinhom alav bayom hahu kenahamat yam*. Another example, Isa 24:19–20, describes an earthquake: "The earth is utterly broken / the earth is torn asunder, / the earth is violently shaken. / The earth staggers like a drunkard, / It sway like a hut." In Hebrew, notice the repetition of hard p's and t's, and the cumulative effect of ending each line with "earth" (*arets*). If you practice reading it aloud, you can also pick up the four-beat meter:

> *Ro'ah hitro'e'ah ha'arets*
> *Por hitporerah 'arets*
> *Mot hitmotetah 'arets*
> *No'a tanu'a 'arets*

Also combining several of these untranslatable techniques, Nahum 2:10 pronounces judgment with the words "devastation, desolation, and destruction," which barely does justice to the rolling accumulation of sound in the original: *buqáh umébuqah umebúlaqah*.

Hebrew Poetry Techniques Preserved in Translation

While a glimpse at the ancient poets' facility with their language is interesting, the most important aspects of their writing come through in English translation, and our focus in this part of the text will be to explore how these techniques lead to insights in the psalms, prophets, and wisdom writings of the Old Testament.

Parallelism is repetition, contrast, or completion of an idea by restatement in the next line. We are familiar with this technique, which is often used in music, including these famous lyrics:

"Take me out to the ballgame, take me out with the crowd"

"Silent night, holy night / All is calm, all is bright"

"I feel good, like I knew that I would / I feel nice, like sugar and spice"

Notice that this technique does not involve merely saying the same thing two different ways. In each example above, the second line adds to the first by offering a new image to create a more meaningful whole. Now consider this biblical example, from Isa 1:16–20:

16a Wash yourselves; make yourselves clean;

b remove the evil of your doings

c from before my eyes;

d cease to do evil,

17a learn to do good;

b seek justice,

c rescue the oppressed,

d defend the orphan,

e plead for the widow.

18a Come now, let us argue it out, says the Lord:

b though your sins are like scarlet,

c they shall be like snow

d though they be red like crimson,

e they shall become like wool.

19a If you are willing and obedient,

b you shall eat the good of the land;

20a but if you refuse and rebel,

b you shall be devoured by the sword;

c for the mouth of the Lord has spoken.

Close examination reveals several different kinds of parallelism here, which can be broken down as follows:

Synonymous parallelism involves a similar thought conveyed in successive lines. This is the most common poetic technique in the Bible, and this passage from Isaiah gives three common variations on the method: verses 16a and 16b–c at first seem to be two ways of saying the same thing, but 16b–c makes it clearer that the poem concerns morality, not washing, and that God is watching. Verse 17b is a general command to seek justice, while 17c, d, and e specify the recipients. Note that the parallelism here involves three lines instead of the usual two. Verse 18b varies the form a little by skipping a line for its parallel, 18d, while 18c parallels 18e; the strong contrast between red and white, and its repetition, clearly signifies purification by blood.

Antithetic parallelism is an opposition or contrast of thought where the second line expresses the truth of the first in a negative way. Another way to say what something *is,* is to say what it *is not.* Consider the Isaiah example: verses 19a and 20a contrast "willing and obedient" with "refuse and rebel." Verses 19b and 20b contrast "eat the good of the land" with "devoured by the sword."

Climactic parallelism occurs when a line partially repeats and advances the thought of the previous line. This technique is a little more subtle than the first two, so it requires careful consideration of the progression of ideas. The Isaiah passage contains two examples: "Learn to do good" (17a) is not quite the opposite of "cease to do evil" (16d); it requires good actions, beyond the cessation of bad actions.

Synthetic parallelism happens when one line completes the thought of the previous line. Verses 16b and 16c are an example of this, which is technically not parallelism, since nothing in the second line parallels the first, but the units are written as couplets and together form a complete thought.

In almost all instances of parallelism, the word or phrase in the first verset tends to be a standard or common expression, while the word or phrase in the second verset is more unusual, and literary. This pattern serves to intensify the comparison and to add interest.

8a: *Read Psalm 1*, printed below, label the different kinds of parallelism, and comment on how meaning is added, not simply repeated, by slight differences in the lines.

    1a Happy are those

    b who do not follow the advice of the wicked,

    c or take the path that sinners tread,

    d or sit in the seat of scoffers;

    2a but their delight is in the law of the Lord,

    b and on his law they meditate day and night.

    3a They are like trees

    b planted by streams of water,

    c which yield their fruit in its season,

    d and their leaves do not wither.

    e In all that they do, they prosper.

    4a the wicked are not so,

    b But are like chaff that the wind drives away.

    5a Therefore the wicked will not stand in the judgment,

    b nor sinners in the congregation of the righteous;

    6a for the Lord watches over the way of the righteous,

    b but the way of the wicked will perish.

For Further Study:

1. Copy and paste one of the following passages into a computer file, divide the text as above into shorter lines, and label the kinds of parallelism: Psalm 97, Proverbs 17, Isaiah 60.

2. Choose a famous poem written with rhyme and meter (e.g., a Shakespeare sonnet), remove the line breaks, change the non-rhyming words to synonyms, and update the language throughout. What is gained and lost by your "translation"?

3. Choose a contemporary song that uses repetition and parallelism. What is added to the song by this technique, and how important are meter and rhyme to the impact of the song?

4. Find examples in modern music or poetry of the poetry techniques described in the text, or re-write a famous work like the Gettysburg Address employing as many of them as possible.

Chapter 9

Imagery in Hebrew Poetry

Image, Symbol, Metaphor

Poetry packs a lot into a small space, sometimes letting a verbal picture "say a thousand words." In order to be precise, we need to define some of the terms for this technique. Consider the definitions and examples carefully, because we will use these terms extensively from this point on.

An *image* names a concrete thing or action where the *first* level of meaning is primary, and the reader must consider what the image evokes. For example, Ps 8:6–8 lists creatures lower than humanity in the order of creation: sheep, oxen, beasts of the field, birds of the air, and the fish of the sea. None of these images has additional meaning; yet together, the images suggest the size and complexity of the natural world. This evokes wonder and appreciation much more than the use of an abstract word like "creation."

A *symbol* names a concrete thing or action where the *second* level of meaning is primary. For example, in Exodus 19–20, God summons Moses up a mountain covered in smoke and fire in order to reveal to him the Ten Commandments. Smoke, fire, and mountains are real things, and part of the story, but they also symbolize mystery and power; and the mountain symbolizes the difficulty of gaining access to God. Words like light, darkness, water/sea, fire, mountain, and tree are each used hundreds of times in the Bible, often as symbols of larger realities.

You will recall from the earlier description of narrative technique the distinction between *metaphor*, an implied comparison where noun or verb represents something else and *simile*, a comparison that uses the word "like." Both metaphor and simile are a kind of parallelism, consisting of only one word. Biblical examples abound. In the Psalms, God might be called a shepherd (Ps 23, 80), a rock (Ps 31, 62), or a hen (Ps 17, 36, 57). Righteous people are *like* trees (Ps 1, 52, 92); all people in their mortality are *like* grass (Ps 37, 90, 102). Metaphor includes personification, as for example where a nation is spoken of as an individual (Hos 11:1; Isa 42:1; Ezek 23), or nature is spoken of as shouting and clapping (Ps 98, 148). Relations between God and humanity are often described in metaphorical language. The most common of these are king/subject (e.g., Deut 17:14–20; 1 Sam 8:4–18; Isa 6), judge/litigant (e.g., Exod 18:13–27; 2 Sam 12:1–15; Ezra 7:25–28), husband/wife (e.g., Jer 3:1–5; Ezek 23; Hosea 1–3; Eph

5:21–25; Rev 21), father/child (e.g., Gen 21; 1 Sam 2:29–34; Matt 6; Rom 5:12–14), and master/servant (e.g., Gen 18; 1 Kings 8; Mal 1:6; Matt 20; John 13).

The use of metaphor introduces the difficult question of God's "gender." There are more than a dozen feminine metaphors for God in the Old Testament, most often characterizing God as a mother (Isa 66:13; Hos 11:3–4) or mother bird (Deut 32:11; Ps 57:1) who gives birth and nourishes or protects her children. In the New Testament, similarly, Jesus refers to God as a hen who longs to gather her children under her wings (Matt 23:37; Luke 13:34). Do these passages challenge the traditional assumption that God is male? Some might respond that such relatively infrequent references involve "poetic license," whereas the overwhelming number of biblical images for God, as well as the names, verb forms, and pronouns used by biblical writers, are male. But if God is spirit and does not have a body—as biblical writers clearly believed—doesn't that imply that the *male* imagery and word forms equally involve "poetic license"? Furthermore, the biblical term *spirit* is feminine in Hebrew and neuter in Greek, and the word is frequently used for God's Spirit—but translated into English with a male pronoun! Confusing? The fact is, neither biblical writers nor we have a pronoun for a fourth, "divine" gender; we are limited to *he*, *she*, or *it*. Under the recent influence of feminism, some now use *she* for God or at least for God's Spirit; others use *he* and *she* together or alternately, and some propose a new, gender-neutral pronoun. This text addresses—or sidesteps?—the issue as some Bible translations and hymnals do, by avoiding pronouns for God altogether. Readers may wish to pursue further the theological and cultural issues of God and gender, which we touch upon here only as an offshoot of the consideration of metaphor.

Why are metaphor and simile so common, when a straightforward statement might convey the author's intention more directly? For the same reason that biblical storytellers rarely explain the point of their stories. Use of metaphor invites the reader to ponder, and more importantly, to become involved in the discovery of a truth. As a technique, use of metaphor shows respect for the audience, coaxing the reader toward insight and allowing different people to discover different shades of meaning. Of course, like an approachable and gentle person, metaphor may attract both admirers and opportunists, and interpretations may be insightful or outlandish. Still, from a literary point of view, the genius of this and several other common forms of biblical writing (narrative, gospel, parable) is that they encourage the very participation in discovery and growth that is the hallmark of the Bible's message. In other words, the medium is often the message.

Archetypes

An *archetype* is a recurring image, symbol, or pattern representing the universal elements of human experience. The words "recurring" and "universal" are keys here. There are certain pictures and basic story lines that appear to be common to virtually every culture and every individual, even to the subconscious mind in the form of dream material. Archetypes were present before the Bible was written and will always accompany humanity. This helps to explain the capacity of biblical stories and poetry to remain understandable and appealing across the distances of time, culture, and language. Archetypes are so important to the Bible, in fact, that they merit a more detailed treatment here.

It is useful to distinguish between archetypal *images* and archetypal *plots*. Archetypal images may be subdivided into those pertaining to the natural world, those involving human relations or characters, and those of the supernatural world. Each of these categories of images in turn may be understood in terms of ideal and anti-ideal: opposites that tend to imply each other. That is, when an ideal image like a garden appears, the reader can infer that its opposite, a wilderness, is anti-ideal. The table below pairs many of these biblical ideal and anti-ideal archetypal images:

Archetypes in the Bible

Natural World Ideal	*Anti-ideal*
light, sun, moon, stars, sunrise, day, summer	dark, clouds, dusk, night, winter
green grass, rose, vineyard, fruit, tree, lily, grain, sweet taste	dry grass, thistle, weeds, chaff (of grain), bitter taste or poison
garden, mountaintop, hilltop, straight road	wilderness, forest, dark valley, cave, crooked or uphill path
river, spring, rain, dew, tranquil pool	sea, sea monster, drought
sheep, lamb, cattle, dove, hen	predator, lion, snake, goat, eagle
jewels, gold, silver, bright color	dust, ashes, stones, rust, destructive fire
Human Relations or Character Ideal	*Anti-ideal*
community, tribe, city	anarchy, isolation, captivity, slavery, wandering
wedding, marriage, sons, daughters	widow, orphan, cripple, barrenness
feast, family meal, wine, bread	hunger, poison, drunkenness, famine
covenant, treaty	discord, war
palace, fortress, walls, temple, house	prison, wicked city, wilderness
stately, festal, or fine garments, armor	ill-fitting, dirty, coarse garments, sackcloth
hero: one who embodies national/religious beliefs, achieves against opposition	failure due to character flaw, following idols
scapegoat: one who is punished unjustly to save others (no anti-ideal)	
trickster: one who uses wits to overcome obstacles (no anti-ideal)	
Supernatural World Ideal	*Anti-ideal*
God	Satan, serpent
angel	demon, monsters
heavenly council	false gods, idols

Along with these archetypal images, biblical literature contains archetypal *plots*: universal, recurrent story lines that reflect common human experience. The most common of these are described below:

The *quest* involves a hero's search to reach a goal. There are opponents and helpers along the way, setbacks or temporary defeat, and ultimate success. Examples include Abraham becoming the father of the Jewish nation and the Israelites reaching the Promised Land.

In the *death/rebirth* plot, a hero experiences death (Jesus), near-death (Job), or symbolic death (Israel in exile, Jonah in the fish). This archetype also applies to childbearing after a period of barrenness (Abraham).

The *journey* plot differs from quest in that there is no particular goal, but the character grows through change of place and circumstances. Joseph and David are good examples of development from clever opportunists to wise and humble leaders.

In the *initiation* plot, a character is forced out of an ideal situation and must learn something new. Joseph must respond to imprisonment, Israel must learn obedience in the wilderness or in exile.

A *comedy* plot does not involve humor but movement through crisis to new life, family, and community. Each of the patriarchs, and the exodus from Egypt, are comedies in this sense.

A *tragedy* involves a fundamental flaw in a character that results in death and destruction. Adam and Eve are the original and classic example, as are many of the Israelite kings, beginning with Saul.

A *temptation* plot involves a protagonist who encounters an evil figure, with positive or negative results depending on the person's choice. Examples abound, but the most familiar are Adam, David, and Jesus.

The *rags-to-riches* plot, or Cinderella story, is exemplified by Joseph, Job, David, and the nation of Israel itself.

The *liberation* plot involves an individual or group leaving the security of the old order to emerge on a better life path. Biblical examples include Abram reaching the Promised Land, the Israelites leaving Egypt, the transformation of the disciples of Jesus, and Paul changing from persecutor to apostle.

Archetypal plots may be considered in conjunction with archetypal images. An example is the crossing of a body of water, which combines both the idea of water as a symbol of chaos and the quest as symbol of goal achievement. Such a combination adds the sense of finality or irreversibility to the arrival at a goal, a notion doubly or even triply affirmed when the Israelites cross the archetypal barriers of Red Sea, the wilderness, and (most importantly) the Jordan River to enter the Promised Land. Modern examples include Washington crossing the Delaware, or anti-ideals in the *Titanic* and *Lusitania*.

Functions of Archetypes

The examples of archetypal images and plots should seem so familiar as hardly to require explanation, because of course they are all around us in literature, music, films, experiences, and dreams. Their use in the Bible helps to provide order, to fit the categories of experience into patterns. This in turn helps the reader to know what to strive for, how to behave, and what is likely to happen as a result of good choices.

To break down just one category into its constituent parts, consider the initiation plot applied to a familiar story like Snow White. The *hero* experiences *separation* when she is banished to the forest, a lonely orphan. There she undergoes a *struggle* for survival, with the huntsman, woodland creatures, and dwarves as *helpers*; the dangerous forest and wicked queen are her archetypal *opponents*. When she is poisoned, the situation looks grim, but the dwarves watch over her until the prince appears to *return* her to life, a *gift of new power* as he takes her to his father's kingdom as his wife. If my telling of the story here sounds more theological than the film versions of the story, that is because the brothers Grimm intentionally crafted their version of the tale as a Christian allegory, where the "fall" (Snow White's consumption of the apple) is redeemed not by the Prince's kiss but by his dislodging of the piece of apple caught in her throat (sin, source of death) and welcoming her as bride to his father's kingdom (New Testament language for believers entering heaven).

We might apply the same archetypal plot analysis to the partriarch Joseph in Genesis. Left to die by his jealous brothers, he *struggles* to survive as a virtual orphan against *opponents* like the wilderness, Pharoah, and Potiphar's wife; his chief *helper* is God. Joseph *returns* from prison and receives a *gift of new power* to become a high official in Egypt. His brothers appear again, but Joseph is no longer the vain youth, and he uses his trickster skills to save and reunite with his family.

Note that archetypal images—in this case wilderness, orphan, trickster, and marriage—are often part of an archetypal plot. In biblical writings like the Psalms and prophetic writings, where we are unlikely to encounter plots (except indirectly when reference is made to stories of Israel's past), the focus is upon images. As you encounter these images in biblical texts, keep in mind the ideal/anti-ideal scheme, which means that the presence of any image implies its opposite. That is, the biblical writer need only supply one side of the contrast (lion, wilderness, isolation) to stimulate the imagination to supply the other side (lamb, garden, community).

Acknowledgments:

The material above on biblical archetypes relies heavily on Leland Ryken's *Words of Delight: A Literary Introduction to the Bible.* Grand Rapids: Baker, 1992. Pp. 26–29, 48–51.

For Further Study:

1. Discuss the implications of the male-dominant metaphors for God in both historic and contemporary terms. Does patriarchal imagery inevitably lead to patriarchal attitudes and actions?
2. Compose a myth or fairy tale using as many biblical archetypes as possible.
3. Name a famous film or modern novel that exemplifies each of the archetypal plot categories.
4. Which archetypes figure most importantly in your dreams, favorite art works (e.g., images, songs, fiction), and beliefs? Can you draw any connections between these three categories in your own experience?

Chapter 10

From Lament to Praise in the Book of Psalms

Scholars differ in their opinion about the authorship and date of writing of The Book of Psalms. Almost half of the psalms are attributed to David, who was known as a musician (2 Sam 1, 22, 23); eleven are attributed to "the sons of Korah," twelve to "Asaph," a few to other individuals, and many are anonymous. Some scholars dispute direct authorship by David, contending that ascription to him was meant to honor him, not to commit forgery, and that the collection must have been edited over hundreds of years before the Hebrew canon was fixed late in the first century AD. Jewish and Christian tradition, however, maintain that David was the primary author.

The collection is divided into five parts (ending with Ps 41, 72, 89, 106, and 150), perhaps reflecting the fivefold division of the Pentateuch; but there does not appear to be a systematic arrangement within or between these divisions. The most common type is the psalm of *supplication* or request (e.g., 3, 4, 17, 26, 28, 40, 55, 69, 86), which makes up about one third of the total. Next in frequency are psalms of *praise* (e.g., 18, 30, 33, 65, 66, 96, 97, 103, 107, 124, 136, 139, 149), which constitute a little less than a third of the total. Of the remaining third, the most common is the *lament* (10, 13, 22, 35, 38, 51, 54, 64, 74, 77); considered by some a sub-type of the supplication, the lament involves a complaint that culminates in an affirmation of faith. The *pilgrim* psalm or "psalm of ascents" (24, 48, 84, 120–134) is meant to be sung during a journey to the Jerusalem temple; the *royal* psalm (2, 18, 21, 45, 72, 89, 101, 110, 141) deals with kings; the *historical* psalm (68, 78, 105, 106, 135, 136) recapitulates God's acts in history.

We will take a closer look at examples of each of the first three kinds: two psalms of supplication (25, 90), two of praise (19, 103), and two of lament (22, 77). These choices leave out some familiar favorites like Ps 23, 51, and 139, but we will consider representative types of similar length. For each category, you will apply what you have already learned about form and imagery. By studying three pairs of examples representing the most common kinds of psalms, you will become familiar with the techniques behind the vast majority of the psalms, the prophets, and other biblical poetic writing.

Read Psalms 25 and 90

10a: These psalms of supplication stress both behavior and attitude on the part of both God and the one praying. For each psalm, choose three behaviors or attitudes, identify the verses where they are found, and describe how parallelism helps to clarify the message.

Read Psalms 19 and 103

10b: C. S. Lewis, a literary scholar at Oxford, called Psalm 19 "the greatest poem in the Psalter and one of the greatest lyrics in the world." Note the progression from the natural world, to God's revelation of himself, and finally to the author's response. For each of the three sections, and then for the psalm as a whole, comment on the sense of forward movement (climactic parallelism). Then consider Psalm 103 and describe its organization.

Read Psalms 22 and 77

10c: Jesus quotes Psalm 22 from the cross, and a few of its specific images are reflected in his suffering. We will discuss this kind of passage later in relation to prophecy, but for now we will consider it as a psalm of lament. Such psalms include a common sequence of features: appeal to God, complaint, request, statement of confidence in God, vow to praise or obey God. Human laments don't normally end on such a positive note—at least not right away—but many psalms of lament are intended to show a redemptive process. For both psalms, identify the verses that contain the five features in the sequence, and then discuss how despair is conveyed through parallelism.

For Further Study:

1. Choosing one of the three categories considered above, study at least three more examples and look for similarities and differences within the category.

2. Choose one of the subcategories not considered above and describe common features of at least two examples: the *pilgrim* psalm (24, 48, 84, 120–134), the *royal* psalm (2, 18, 21, 45, 72, 89, 101, 110, 141), and the *historical* psalm (68, 78, 105, 106, 135, 136).

3. Discuss the variety of tone (mood or emotion) in the Psalms. What tone or tones predominate? What do you make of sudden shifts in tone within individual psalms?

4. Most readers find the psalms the most personal, or intimate, part of the Bible. Is this entirely due to tone, or are there other techniques that contribute to this assessment?

Chapter 11

The Prophets Speak for God

In the Old Testament, the historical books after the Pentateuch are sometimes called the Former Prophets; they include the prophetic work of figures like Moses, Samuel, and Nathan, none of whom wrote separate books of prophecy. But what is prophecy? Most of us associate the term with predictions of the future, but this is not, technically, the biblical definition. Material in the Bible pertaining to the end of time is a different kind of writing called *apocalyptic*, which we will consider later in this text. In the understanding of biblical writers, a prophet is simply a *spokesman for God*, and this function as mouthpiece may or may not involve statements about the future. In fact, prophetic activity most often involves interpretation of current events, and its dominant themes are justice toward the outcast and loyalty to God.

A distinctive feature of prophetic literature is the *oracle*: a passage that begins, "The word of the Lord." This form occurs more than three hundred times in the Old Testament. An oracle may be further subdivided by type: *judgment, warning,* or *promise*. In all three categories, a statement is followed by an explanation based on God's standards of justice, righteousness, or mercy.

The Old Testament books devoted to prophetic writing do not occur in chronological order, so it is helpful to see them listed by time period, including the relevant history as recorded in 2 Kings:

Timeline of Old Testament Prophetic Books

Prophetic book	Period covered	Narrative account
Joel	835? Unknown	2 Kings 9–12
Jonah	760	2 Kings 14
Amos	760	2 Kings 14
Micah	750	2 Kings 14–20
Hosea	745	2 Kings 14
Isaiah	738–700, 586–520	2 Kings 15–20
Nahum	625–610	2 Kings 22–25

Zephaniah	625	2 Kings 22–25
Jeremiah	620–585	2 Kings 22–25
Habakkuk	615–598	2 Kings 22–25
Lamentations	600	2 Kings 22–25
Obadiah	600	2 Kings 22–25
Ezekiel	592–570	2 Kings 24–25
Daniel	590	2 Kings 24–25
Haggai	520	2 Kings 24–25
Zechariah	520–518	2 Kings 24–25
Malachi	486–450	2 Kings 24–25

The prophetic books are not easy to read. Although our study of psalms makes us familiar with biblical imagery and poetic style, the prophetic books present new challenges. Prophets change topic abruptly and often make reference to the political powers of the time, which are obscure to us. This raises the question: why read this material today?

First, the prophetic books fill in much of the record of the narrative histories, helping us to understand why certain events occurred. That is, while 2 Kings may tell us that a certain king, or the people in general, "did what was evil in the sight of the Lord," the prophetic book that coincides with this period spells out the issues in graphic detail with accounts of idol worship and social injustice. A second reason to read the prophetic books is that they contain details that were either unfulfilled at the time of writing or that later interpreters, including New Testament writers, understood in connection with the future hopes of Israel, including the messiah—and for Christians, Jesus himself. A third reason to consider the prophetic books is that they reveal biblical priorities. That is, admonitions and condemnations reveal the kinds of behavior that God approves, while promises of mercy and restoration reveal God's character. Indeed, although the prophetic oracles were addressed to particular situations, their status as "the word of the Lord" gives them a timeless element recognized by other biblical writers and by generations of believers. Thus, ironically, to study the often-obscure prophetic material makes historic Jewish and Christian belief clearer.

From a literary perspective, we might add a fourth reason to study the prophets. There is a distinct *tone,* or emotional atmosphere, in these writings unlike anything else in the Bible. Much of the Bible reports events or describes doctrine and morality with almost no reference to emotions. Although ancient people undoubtedly experienced feelings like ours, they did not have the language of modern psychology that is familiar to us. Nevertheless, we value tone in literature because it is a way of inviting us into the inner world of the writer, when we not only think but feel in response to the words. Emotion is often conveyed in biblical poetry, but the prophetic writings are dominated by tone. In the following pages, you will consider for yourself the tone of these writings.

Approaching the Bible as Literature
Interlude: The Prophets and Social Justice

Throughout the prophetic writings—and elsewhere in the Old Testament—the people of God are commanded to care for those who are at a social disadvantage: widows, orphans, the poor (which includes the sick or injured, who have no means of support), and strangers (non-Israelites). Inspired in part by this ancient tradition, modern societies have expanded these categories, but the principle remains the same. We observe, however, that "altruism," or giving to others who cannot repay, contradicts the principle of survival of the fittest. Where did social justice originate? Anthropologists speculate that in pre-literary cultures, property was not shared but owned by the chief or head of the group. In order to preserve his position and that of his dependents and descendants after his death, he was obligated to provide from his bounty for the needs of those who experienced deprivation or loss. A more crude way of putting this is, "As long the chief has plenty, you will all have enough." As tribes expanded to nations this principle applied not only to chiefs or kings but to anyone with high socio-economic status. Religious authorities, from shamans in tribes to high priests in more advanced social systems, guarded this arrangement to ensure its consistent application over time; and of course the sanction of the god(s) strengthened the mandate. It is easy to understand, therefore, how the performance of justice became critical to the individual's and the nation's relationship with God long before the expression of more abstract virtues like love, patience, and humility. In fact, it might be argued that the qualities that we call virtues in some sense grew from notions of social justice: a person who is kind toward the poor is usually kind in general, and vice versa. This relationship between justice and virtue may also help to understand the developing recognition that God is not simply all-powerful but also all-providing and, therefore, kind, loving, patient, etc.

The command to provide justice for widows, orphans, and the poor is common in ancient Near Eastern documents from Egypt and Babylon that pre-date the Old Testament. In the Pentateuch, attention to the needs of these groups is common (Exod 22:22–25; Deut 15:4—16:11; 26:12), and neglect of the widow, orphan, and poor form the basis for prophetic pronouncements (Isa 9:17, Ezek 16:49, Hos 14:3). The addition of the alien or foreigner (Exod 22:21, Deut 10:19, Jer 7:6, Zech 7:10, Mal 3:5), along with the explicit command to make non-discriminatory laws (Exod 22:49, Num 9:14, Deut 23:7) is a contribution on the part of Old Testament writers based explicitly on the principle of empathy: "You shall not oppress a resident alien . . . for you were aliens in the land of Egypt" (Exod 23:9, Deut 23:7). This notion eventually emerges in commands to show kindness even to enemies (Exod 23:4–5, Prov 24:17, 25:21, 29:10); in the New Testament, it lies behind Jesus' command to love one's enemies (Matt 5:43–45, Luke 6:27–28; cf. Rom 12:12, 20). Thus the original demands for social justice remain an important aspect of the Judeo-Christian ethical tradition, but over time they also become more inclusive, radical, abstract, and perhaps more difficult to measure.

This ambiguity, from a literary perspective, is consistent with the narrative ambiguity we have already encountered as well as that of forms we are yet to consider: wisdom, gospel, parable, and apocalyptic. Significantly, it appears that the more advanced the religious development, the more complex and open to interpretation the literature.

We will consider two prophetic books: Isaiah, which is typical of the Old Testament prophetic literature; and Jonah, which has a style and issues all its own.

Isaiah in Historical Context

Isaiah of Jerusalem was active in the late eighth century BC, a period recorded in 2 Kings 15–20 which describes the decline of the divided kingdoms of Israel and Judah under the shadow of the fading but still-mighty Assyrian empire. Isaiah saw the fall of the northern kingdom of Israel, the destruction of its capital city, Samaria, and the exile of its leaders. Despite the seeming invincibility of the Assyrians, Isaiah advised the good king of Judah, Hezekiah, to defy the Assyrian emperor Sennacharib; miraculously, the Jews were successful. Not long after the death of Hezekiah, however, the kingdom of Judah fell to the rising Babylonian empire, and we know nothing about what happened to Isaiah. The book that bears his name is usually divided into two or three sections, and most scholars attribute only the first of these (chapters 1–39) to Isaiah of Jerusalem. This is because from chapter 40, references are made to specific events and names from the end of the Babylonian exile, more than one hundred years after Isaiah's time. As a result, many scholars suggest that this section was written by a later author, perhaps another prophet, in Isaiah's name. For our purposes, however, issues regarding date and authorship are secondary to the style and themes revealed in these passages.

Kinds of Prophecy

We observed earlier that biblical prophecy does not necessarily predict the future. There are in fact four distinct kinds of prophecy that we observe in both Old and New Testament books.

Interpretive prophecy gives God's perspective on current events, often beginning with the oracle formula "thus says the Lord." Major themes of interpretive prophecy include idolatry (worship of false gods) and social justice: care for the poor and disadvantaged.

Predictive prophecy foretells the future. This category is sometimes subdivided into two forms: *contemporary predictive* and *future predictive*. The former category, which is most common, predicts events that will occur in the near future, within months or years, and certainly within the lifetime of the writer's audience. The latter category, which predicts "some day" hopes or dangers, is less common. Future predictive prophecy is the most difficult to understand because it often contains symbolic images, events, and numbers that are unclear to modern readers. To add a layer of complication, some interpreters adopt an *already/not yet* distinction for some predictive prophecy, contending that the biblical writer's prediction was partially fulfilled (contemporary predictive) in biblical times and awaits complete fulfillment (future predictive) at some future time. It is beyond the scope of this book to explain further the complexities and controversies associated with predictive prophecy; it is enough for our purposes simply to introduce the kinds of prophetic material present in the Bible.

Typological prophecy involves the use of a symbol or figure from past writing to interpret current events. With this kind of prophecy, it is critical to understand that the prophetic element depends entirely on the second writer. This is common in New Testament writers' use of details from the Old Testament as *types* corresponding to events in the life of Jesus. Examples include the enthronement of

King David (Psalm 110) as a type of Jesus' ascension into heaven (Acts 2:35); and the briefly referenced priest Melchizedek (Gen 18:14, Ps 110:4), who becomes a New Testament type of Christ (Hebrews 5–7). Jesus himself uses typological prophecy in comparing Jonah's three days in the belly of the fish to his death and resurrection (Matt 12:38–42), and when he quotes David's cry of desolation (Psalm 22) from the cross (Mark 15:34).

One famous example of typological prophecy that has proven needlessly controversial is the quotation of Isa 7:14 in Matt 1:23, "Behold, a young maiden (KJV, "virgin") will conceive and bear a son." The original Hebrew in Isaiah reads "young maiden," while Matthew quotes the Greek version of the Old Testament, which uses the word "virgin." The original context was not a future predictive prophecy but a contemporary predictive prophecy designed to bolster the faith of King Ahaz that his royal line would continue. Some believers insist that Isaiah foresaw the birth of Jesus; skeptics respond that such an interpretation defies credibility. With a proper understanding of typological prophecy, however, there is no need to suppose that the prophet Isaiah was thinking about the virgin birth of Jesus eight hundred years in advance or—this is crucial—that Matthew construed Isaiah's words as future predictive. Rather, Matthew perceived the entire Old Testament as a rich source of types, or correspondences. Whether Jesus and New Testament writers were justified in this approach is a matter of *faith*. As a matter of *literary study*, however, typological prophecy is simply a category.

Read Isaiah 1–11

11a: What are two similarities between the writing in these chapters and the psalms? What are two important differences? Explain.

11b: If you were to write a guide to righteous living based on Isaiah 1–11, what would be the two or three most important behaviors? Give examples to defend your position.

11c: What is the tone (attitude or emotional atmosphere) in most of the prophecies in chapters 1–10, and how does it differ from the tone in chapter 11? Quote a phrase or two from each section to support your response.

Read Isaiah 51–66

11d: These chapters address the people during their exile in Babylon, recognizing their suffering and promising them future comfort. Does the moral teaching remain the same or differ from what you read in chapters 1–11? Give a few examples to support your position.

11e: Isaiah 53 is considered by Christians to be a reference to Jesus (see Acts 8:26–35), but Jews see it as Israel personified. Give the strongest argument for each position.

11f: Isaiah 60–66 contain a strong message of hope. Choose one passage of at least four lines that you find particularly effective and describe how the imagery and/or parallelism work.

Jonah as Satire?

The book of Jonah, which is included among the prophets in both Jewish and Christian Bibles, is unique in that it contains a story *about* a prophet instead of God's messages *through* the prophet. It is also unusual in that interpreters have long disagreed about whether it was originally intended to be taken as history or as another form of writing. Of course, the most famous incident in the book involves Jonah's three days inside a great fish, which would not be possible except for a miracle. But many scholars, including some who accept the miraculous element, still think that Jonah is a kind of satire or parable, based on features of the book's style and content.

Satire pokes fun at human folly, often using irony and exaggeration. We are familiar with this style from television shows like Saturday Night Live and South Park, but if someone were to watch these shows two hundred years from now—much less two thousand years from now—they would certainly miss most of the humor. Likewise, many readers pass over or take for granted some of the details that suggest Jonah as a comic figure. Examples include Jonah's ridiculous attempt to escape God on a boat, the king of Ninevah's requirement that everyone—including *animals*—must repent, and Jonah's camping outside the city afterward, hoping God will change his mind and destroy it. Furthermore, there is no historical record of any "repentance" in the Assyrian capitol, which in any case was a fraction of the gigantic size described here (3:3). Such details suggest that the story may not have been intended to be taken as history in the first place. Whatever their conclusions about the issue of historicity, interpreters agree that this little book is a literary masterpiece and one of the most entertaining stories in the Bible.

Read Jonah 1–4

11g: What is nonsensical or ridiculous about Jonah's reaction in 4:1–3?

11h: What is nonsensical or ridiculous about Jonah's reaction in 4:8–9?

11i: In 4:10–11, God delivers a clear "moral of the story" in terms of Israel's relations to its neighbors. How does this compare to the message of judgment that you have seen in Psalms and especially in Isaiah?

11j: How might the book of Jonah be described from an archetypal approach?

Other Old Testament Prophetic Books

Because we have considered only two of many Old Testament prophetic books, it is important at least to summarize the others. Along with Isaiah, the two other major prophetic works are Jeremiah and Ezekiel. The heavily poetic *Jeremiah* treats the period just prior to the Babylonian exile (627–582 BC), explaining the coming disaster in terms of the nation's idolatry. The short book of *Lamentations* that follows Jeremiah is also attributed to the prophet. *Ezekiel*, written for the Jews in exile, includes a series of symbol-rich visions and extended metaphors in addition to poetry; it promises judgement to the nations and promises restoration to Jews who will purify themselves and return to the ways of God.

Daniel, which appears next in canonical order, contains both dramatic narrative and visionary, symbolic predictions of future judgment. After Daniel are the so-called Minor Prophets. These twelve short books overlap the longer prophetic works historically, from *Joel*, who may have written as early as the ninth century BC, to *Malachi*, who wrote about 450 BC to announce coming redemption through a messiah. In terms of style and theme, the differences between these books are, in fact, "minor": all address similar issues of disobedience, idolatry, and judgment; all are highly rich in imagery and composed almost entirely in poetry. The exception to this pattern is Jonah, which, as we have seen, merits special consideration and perhaps different characterization.

Approaching the Bible as Literature

For Further Study:

1. What other modern virtues or causes might be linked to beginnings in social justice or Old Testament values, and are there virtues or causes that resist this link?

2. Research Greco-Roman virtues. How might Western culture have developed differently if these ethical norms had prevailed over Judeo-Christian norms? Or *did* they?

3. Ezekiel is another major prophetic work with much greater attention to imagery and archetypes. Consider the description of God in chapter 1, the story of God as lover in chapter 16, or the "dry bones" prediction of chapter 37, and discuss not what the details *describe* but what they *evoke*.

4. Consider one of the minor prophets—Joel, Amos, Micah, or Hosea—and remember that they were written *before* Isaiah. What similarities or differences of technique or content do you see?

5. The book of Daniel is well known but also controversial in terms of authorship and date of writing. How does it differ from other prophetic books? Does the narrative portion seem more like the patriarchal narratives or like Jonah? Does the stress appear to lie on predictions of the future or on righteous behavior?

6. Read Malachi and comment on how it both reiterates familiar themes and reinforces the notion of continuous movement forward in the prophetic literature.

Chapter 12

Pondering Imponderables in Wisdom Literature

As we read earlier, the ancient Jews first recognized the Pentateuch, then other works of history and prophecy, to form "the law and the prophets." The last group of books, known as the Writings, are as miscellaneous as the name implies. They include history (Ruth, 1–2 Chronicles, Esther, Ezra-Nehemiah), poetry (Psalms, Song of Solomon), prophecy (Lamentations, Daniel), and what is known as *wisdom literature*, the content of which focuses on the meaning of life and appropriate conduct.

The biblical books that constitute wisdom literature vary in form of writing. Job is mostly poetry, Proverbs contains short sayings, and Ecclesiastes is an essay with a few poems. What these three books have in common is a perspective entirely unlike anything else in the Bible. They appear to be written by and for members of the educated, ruling elite: those who have the time and sophistication to consider the purpose of suffering, the fine points of morality, and the meaning of life. There appears to be little interest here in the dominant themes we have encountered up to now in the Old Testament: laws and purity codes that distinguish God's people from the surrounding cultures, recognition of God's help and mercy in times of trouble, the nation's history, and concerns about justice for the downtrodden. Instead, these books stress order, which is aligned with goodness, as opposed to chaos, which is aligned with folly. The fuller picture of ancient Judaism provided by wisdom literature prevents generalizations about "the law and the prophets." Biblical content is simply too diverse for generalization.

Job Happens

Suggestions concerning an author and date for the book of Job are all over the map, and perhaps beside the point, given the timeless nature of the message. Bad things happen to a good person, his so-called friends offer questionable advice, God finally speaks, and then things get even more challenging. From a literary perspective, scholars agree that this is a masterfully crafted work, with a rich vocabulary, tidy organization, dramatic dialogue, powerful poetry, and just enough ambiguity to keep people discussing it for three thousand years.

After the prose prologue in the first two chapters, a series of speeches follows in which Job's friends weigh in three times. Each time, the friends express the traditional belief that Job must have done something terrible to merit such suffering, while Job rightly insists that he is innocent. This is dramatic irony; the reader knows (from the prologue) that Job is innocent. After the rounds of speeches, there is a poetic interlude, then a series of monologues (one speaker): by Job, by a fourth friend, and by God. Finally, Job responds to God's speech, and then the story wraps up with a brief prose page. Study the diagram below of the book's structure before reading further.

The Structure of Job

Prologue   1–2

Speeches   3—42:6

Dialogues   3–27

     Job's opening lament   3

     Dialogue in three cycles   4–27

     Eliphaz / Job   4–7, 15–17, 22–25

     Bildad / Job   8–10, 18–19, 25–27

     Zophar / Job   11–14, 20–21

Poem on wisdom   28

Monologues   29–41

     Job   29–31

     Elihu   32–37

     God   38–41

     Job   42

Epilogue   42:7–17

We will consider only the first cycle of dialogues, which is enough to get a flavor for the central section; then we will jump ahead to God's speech near the end of the book. While reading the speeches of Job's friends, look for the conventional view of God's justice. From a child's first lament, "That's not fair!" and from all cultures and periods of history, there is a strong human compulsion to match what happens with what is deserved. How do we integrate this impulse with our belief in events with no cause or events with a divine cause? Is it true that "everything happens for a reason," or do we make up reasons to fit situations—and if so, is that wrong? Our answers to such questions—especially in crisis—are both character forming and character revealing. Such is the timeless subject of the Book of Job.

Read Job 1–14

12a: Choose a few lines that you think represent the strongest argument on the part of one of Job's friends, and explain why you think it is persuasive.

12b: In terms of the way the book is structured, consider why there are three friends, not one and not four or more. What purpose is achieved by having three friends in dialogue with Job?

Read Job 38–42

12c: If you read what leads up to God's speech, you may be surprised by how abrupt it is. God does not responding directly to anything that has been said up to this point. Instead, God appears to change the subject, describing some of the wonders of creation, including the mythical, heavily stylized Behemoth (hippopotamus) and Leviathan (crocodile).

What, in your view, is the point of answering Job with a description of creation rather than an explanation of justice?

12D: Comment on Job's response in 42:1–6. Is he saying that his questions have been answered, that he is overwhelmed by a fuller understanding of God's power, that he is finally convinced that he deserves his suffering, or something else?

Understanding the Book of Job

Since we know from the prologue that Job is innocent, the extended series of dialogues between Job and his so-called friends may be ironic. Here is a classic threefold structure—Job speaks, his friends respond, again and again and again—but the pattern leads nowhere. After all the talk, Job still maintains his innocence, and his friends maintain their "correct" theological accusations.

Then God speaks (ch 38–41), changing the subject of the conversation. Instead of discussing justice, God describes his own creative powers in all their complexity and mystery, essentially asserting that no one can comprehend his purposes. It is absurd, the book suggests, to criticize God's supervision of human events from the standpoint of human reason or standards of justice. But even here, the ideas are conveyed in poetry rather than in rational propositions. The book's point is to invite the reader to work out the truth; God refuses to be a moral accountant.

Job's response (ch 42) to the idea that God cannot be reduced to rational or even ethical categories is dramatic: Job is humbled. After all the talk that fills the book, one sentence from Job suffices: "I had heard of you by the hearing of the ear, but now my eye sees you; therefore I despise myself and repent in dust and ashes" (42:5–6). This may have been no more satisfying to ancient readers than it is to modern Western readers. We want more from God, or we may want protagonists who are proud and defiant. But from a *literary* point of view, the ideas are sifted and funneled from the meandering, road-to-nowhere speculation of Job and his friends (typical of human theological debate?), to the pointed assertion of God's power and mystery, and finally to Job's brief "I get it" response.

But wait! There's more. The last paragraphs (42:7–17) depart from poetry and inform us that Job is restored to health, prosperity, and a new family. Some scholars have complained that the ending is awkward, that the closing paragraph contradicts the message by suggesting that Job is being rewarded for good behavior, and that this section may have been added later by someone uncomfortable with the poetic ambiguity up to that point. Other scholars, particularly literary critics, regard the prose ending as fitting and necessary. The Adversary in the divine council (ch 1–2) has lost his wager, which makes this prose ending a perfect complement to the prose beginning. Job has not rejected God, nor has he ever expressed regret for having lived righteously, and the book never suggests that Job was being rewarded for righteousness. The conclusion is consistent with the message: God doesn't reward Job for being *good*, but for being *humble*.

The overall message of the Book of Job is that we should not infer sin from suffering, much less think of suffering as God's punishment. The book is a classic expression of the longing for divine order, which is baffled but never stopped by the chaos of real life. Why express this in verse? Poetry was the form taken by seekers of wisdom in the ancient Near East. Since it engages the imagination and emotions, it is the appropriate mode for the kind of persuasion that goes beyond intellect to engage the whole person. Poetry allows stark, untempered expression that causes reflection, leading to new insights. The density of poetic language allows the reader to make process by associative leaps rather than by logical development.

Proverbs as Poetic Advice

The Book of Proverbs begins with ascription to Solomon, who was famous for his wisdom (1 Kings 3–4). The anthology includes other authors, including "the Wise" (24:23–34), Agur son of Jakeh (30), and Lemuel king of Massa (31:1–9); others may have had a hand in shaping the collection over time. Most of the proverbs are crisp, two-line sentences which incorporate parallelism and describe an aspect of experience. The morality is conservative, focusing on order. In some sections, the sayings are grouped by subject, such as general insights about wisdom (1–3), avoidance of infidelity (5–7), and the virtuous wife (31). The majority of the proverbs, however, lack any clear organizational scheme. In order to get a sense of the collection, we will consider a representative section.

Read Proverbs 8–10

12f: What indications do you find here that these proverbs are intended for members of the ruling class?

12g: Choose a proverb of 2–4 lines from these three chapters and describe how the meaning is conveyed by the use of parallelism.

Pondering Imponderables in Wisdom Literature
Ecclesiastes and the Ambiguity of Life

In the first verse, the writer of Ecclesiastes calls himself "the Teacher, son of David," which supports the traditional association with Solomon. Some scholars, however, regard the title as an honorific designation and maintain that the vocabulary and style of the book place it between the fifth and third centuries BC. In terms of content, Ecclesiastes seems to present deliberate tensions and contradictions, moving between faith and doubt, cynicism and hope, practical guidance and despair. It is almost impossible to point to one statement, even the ending, and pronounce, "Here is the point of the book." There are scholars who are equally sure that the message challenges, or denies, traditional faith. Rather than take sides, perhaps it is better simply to appreciate the complexity both of the work itself and of the faith that led ancient Jews to include such a surprising document in their Bible.

Read Ecclesiastes 1–12

12h: Choose a passage that conveys a tone of confusion or despair and comment on how this is achieved by the writing, either in terms of imagery, parallelism, or some other way.

12i: Choose a passage that appears to affirm traditional beliefs and comment on whether, in your view, this is an *exception* to the general message of the book or a *correction* to it.

The Song of Solomon: Erotic Love Poetry or Allegory?

The only Old Testament book not yet mentioned is the Song of Solomon or Song of Songs, which is a short collection of love poetry. Like Proverbs and Ecclesiastes, the content appears to reflect the circumstances of the ruling classes, and it is traditionally attributed to Solomon (who is named in 1:1, 5, 3:7, 9, 11).

The poetry is hard to classify as "wisdom literature," because it does not address concerns about the meaning of life. On the face of it, we are reading highly charged romantic verses, placed in the voices of at least two lovers, between whom a kind of dialogue takes place. The poetry is rich in images and parallelism, and there is no mistaking its sexual content: if this book were a movie, it would be rated R.

So how does a collection of erotic poems end up part of the Bible? Why would the ancient Jews include it along with books of law, prophecy, and history? While we do not have records of the deliberations of the ancient Jews about what to include in the scriptures, we do know that from the earliest records available, the Jews understood this book as an allegory. That is, on the surface the Song of Solomon depicts the love between a young man and a young woman, but it contains hidden truths about God's love for Israel. Later, Christians took up a similar notion, interpreting the book as a symbolic treatment of Christ's love for the Church.

Modern readers may suppose that the ancients were embarrassed by the sexual content and turned the book into something else. But the ancient Jews were quite open about sex, and there were other romances that they did not choose to allegorize or include in the Old Testament. We also know that they were quite familiar with allegory (e.g., Psalm 23, Judges 9, Jeremiah 2, Hosea, Ezekiel 16, 23). The early Christians, similarly, were familiar with the parables of Jesus in the Gospels, and they were accustomed to finding typological prophecy in the Old Testament. In addition, both groups were quite familiar with the notion of God as a husband wooing his people as one would woo a bride. So even though the allegorical interpretation of the Song of Solomon may appear to involve polite avoidance of its apparent meaning, from the perspective of faith, the book may have more than one meaning. In any case, most modern Jews and Christians are happy to enjoy the book simply as love poetry (especially at weddings!), believing that God approves of romance and sex in the appropriate context; while some continue to explore another level of meaning.

The End of the Old Testament

Before moving on to the New Testament, it is important in our treatment of the Bible as *literature* to consider how the Old Testament ends. Although wisdom literature may have been the last written or collected for inclusion in the Old Testament, the Jews of New Testament times had up to that point officially approved only "the law and the prophets." The prophetic collection, which is grouped chronologically, ends with Malachi, who concludes his prophetic message with these words:

> See, I am sending my messenger to prepare the way before me, and the Lord whom you seek will suddenly come to the temple. The messenger of the covenant in whom you delight—indeed, he is coming, says the Lord of hosts. But who can endure the day of his coming, and who can stand when he appears? (Mal 3:1–2)

> Lo, I will send you the prophet Elijah before the great and terrible day of the Lord comes. He will turn the hearts of parents to their children and the hearts of children to their parents, so that I will not come and strike the land with a curse. (Mal 4:5–6)

It is important to understand that these words, written about 450 BC, were the last messages by a prophet to the Jewish people. You may have assumed that there was always a prophet around claiming to have messages from God, but this was not the case. Many Jews during this period believed that the nation needed to increase its own level of righteousness in order to realize its hope for another prophet. By the New Testament period, the Jews had been waiting for centuries—longer than it has been for Americans since the Pilgrims landed on Plymouth Rock. More specifically, the Jews were waiting for a prophet who would represent the great Elijah, whose activities are recorded in 1 Kings 17–21 but who did not write a biblical book. This righteous prophet would prepare God's people to welcome the *messiah* (Hebrew for "anointed"), a new king descended from David who would usher in a golden age.

From a literary perspective, then, it is critical to see that the Old Testament leaves the reader hanging, pointing forward over a long period of time (for many Jews, continuing to this day) toward a hopeful future. It is important to observe this notion built into the content of key books, and also into the very structure of the Old Testament.

Approaching the Bible as Literature

Old Testament Themes and Priorities

Given the diversity of ideas and approaches in the Old Testament, it is useful to summarize some of the important themes and priorities that characterize this substantial literary collection.

The *quest for nationhood* is a critical theme that serves as the organizing principle of the historical books and the subtext of both prophetic writings and psalms. From Genesis through the books of Kings, we observe a series of individual and corporate quests involving finding and then losing an ideal homeland, wandering journeys, dissolution of homogeneity, and return.

A second important theme is the notion of *promise linked to obligation*. This is another way of describing covenant, which is the primary mode of relation between God and his people in the Old Testament. More specifically, God makes promises linked to obligation for humanity in general (Gen 9:1–17), Abraham (Gen 17:7–8), the Hebrews under Moses (Exod 20:22—23:33), and David (2 Sam 7:22–24). The obligation aspect of the covenant is the moral code, given in Exod 20, Deut 5–10, and in a single verse from the prophet Micah: "He has told you, O mortal, what is good; and what does the Lord require of you but to do justice, to love kindness, and to walk humbly with your God?" (Mic 6:8). Justice, kindness, and humility are most often described in terms of care for the downtrodden, especially widows, orphans, the poor, and strangers (foreigners).

The *mercy of God* is a third important Old Testament theme. Although justice demands punishment when an individual or the nation fails to keep their obligation in the covenant, the Old Testament lays the stress on God's kindness and grace rather than his justice. God's people do not always get what they deserve—they get something better. That is, God repeatedly exercises mercy, from the rescue of a remnant from the Flood, to the gift of the Promised Land despite the people's rebellion in the wilderness, to the preservation of the nation despite the corruption of its kings, to the nation's restoration to its homeland despite its exile, and to the hope of a messiah still to come. As Jeremiah puts it, "Thus says the Lord: I have loved you with an everlasting love; therefore I have continued my faithfulness to you" (31:2–3).

A fourth key theme in the Old Testament is *redemptive movement*. Every book is infused with a sense of linear movement toward a better situation. This is evident in the beginning when a promise of ultimate redemption is offered to Adam and Eve after their expulsion from the Garden. It continues through the story of Noah, the Exodus, Israel's nationhood, her return from exile, the pattern of most individual psalms, and in all of the promises in the prophetic literature concerning a redeemer to come in the line of David. However bleak the present, a better reality lies in the future. This fundamentally optimistic view of history and of time is fundamental to the organization of the Bible and to the Jewish and Christian view of the world. As we have seen, it is written into Hebrew poetry, which builds through parallelism to clarity and resolution.

Along with these important themes in the Old Testament, there are also *priorities* for the formation of a perspective toward life and conduct, which some refer to as a "world view." Among the priorities distinctive in the Old Testament is the notion that *God is other than creation*, an idea with far-reaching implications for relations between God, humanity, and the natural world. Another priority is the affirmation of *order emerging from chaos*, which has implications for the way God and nature work and the way humans should act. A third Old Testament priority is the concept of *ethical monotheism*: the one God who created humanity also instructed humanity about how to live. Ethical monotheism began with Judaism; before it there were glimpses of monotheism in different cultures but not an ethical God. A final priority in the Old Testament literature is the *affirmation of mystery*. Pondering the imponderables is built into stories, poetry, and wisdom literature. Truth cannot be reduced to a list of rational propositions; morality cannot be reduced to a neat list of rules. Life is complicated, God is mysterious, people are complex, and even heroes are flawed. In these affirmations, the Old Testament defies the simplistic notion that religion—especially ancient religion—was simply a matter of making oneself pure by observing certain rules and rituals. The Old Testament refuses reduction and invites its readers to insight.

For Further Study:

1. How is Job like and unlike the biblical characters of Joseph, Moses, or David?
2. In what sense is the book of Job a "period piece," and in what sense is it continually relevant?
3. How does the morality of Proverbs either reinforce or conflict with the morality of the prophetic books?
4. In what sense does the description of the ideal wife in Proverbs 31 confirm or deny your presuppositions about the view of women at that time? Is this description affirming or stifling for women today?
5. Compare and contrast the view of life in Ecclesiastes with that of a patriarchal narrative, selected psalms (e.g., 22, 51, 139), or the prophet Joel.
6. Does the dual literal/allegorical use of works like *The Divine Comedy, Alice in Wonderland*, or *The Matrix* make acceptable the same use of the Song of Solomon? How important is the author's original intent to the meaning of a literary work?
7. Ten different writers would probably produce ten different lists of key themes. Based on your reading, what is at least one theme that you would add to this list?
8. What category of biblical writing best conveys each of the categories listed above, and why?
9. Name an important novel that shares at least one of these key themes. Would you argue that the themes are universal, or that there is a strong Judeo-Christian influence on modern literature? Is this likely to change in the future, and why?

Section Four

The Not-So-Silent Silent Years

Chapter 13

The View from the Bridge

A series of world-shaking events occurred during the 450-year period from the end of the last Old Testament prophetic book, Malachi, and the events described in the first New Testament book, Matthew. Although this textbook focuses on literature, not history, the writings of the New Testament are much clearer when seen in relation to developing events and ideas. This section highlights important events that have a bearing on the New Testament story, and it offers an overview of the enormous volume of writing produced between the testaments. As we will see, this period may involve a "gap" in sacred texts, but there is plenty of material from other sources to bridge that gap. The selective "view from the bridge" in this section will serve to set the stage for our consideration of New Testament literature in the sections that follow.

The Peace of Persia

At the end of the Old Testament, the Jews maintained a small, relatively independent realm on the outskirts of the far-flung Persian dominion. Jews commonly spoke the official language of the empire, Aramaic, and Hebrew gradually fell into disuse except in religious contexts. Jewish religion focused on the rebuilt temple, and the Jews' relative isolation led to growing prosperity and religious conservatism focused on obedience to God's law. A class of experts on scripture known as *scribes* emerged to guide interpretation of sacred texts. Some Jews remained behind in Babylon after permission was granted to return to their homeland, beginning a trend of settlements outside Israel that established what has been known ever since as the Jewish *diaspora* (Greek for "dispersion").

Greek Conquest and Culture

Jewish isolation began to end in 333 BC, when Alexander the Great conquered the fading Persian Empire and acquired its territories, including the land occupied by the Jews. There were no battles fought on Jewish soil; in fact, for three hundred years following their return from exile, the Jews were isolated from world conflicts. Nevertheless, Alexander's military conquests left in their wake a far more extensive *cultural* conquest. The Greeks founded new cities and made their way of life, known as *Hellenism*, the standard of acceptability in their new spheres of influence. Their language quickly became the common language of trade, and their standards of culture—religion, architecture, dress, entertainment—grew inexorably in influence. After Alexander's death, the Jews were ruled by the descendants of two of his generals, and pressure built up as the cultural revolution of Hellenism encountered the Jews' own rich and deeply established ethnic heritage.

The Greek language, in a dialect known as *koine* ("common"), was spread by Alexander's soldiers and became the dominant language or *lingua franca* in the Mediterranean world from 300 BC onward. The entire New Testament is written in *koine* Greek, as are most important Christian documents up to about AD 500, when Latin became dominant. The impact of a single language used over a wide geographic area is tremendous. Not only does it bring people closer together by facilitating communication, but it also exerts its own influence on those cultures as its particular style of logic and expression begin to take effect. In short, a language brings with it a new system of thought. For ancient Jews, this clash of thought systems was cataclysmic: West met East, Athens met Jerusalem, Plato met Moses. The questions of when to compromise and when to resist confronted the Jews at every turn, and the variety of answers is reflected in the stormy political and religious developments of the period.

Independence and Tension

In the mid-second century BC, the Jews rebelled against their Greek rulers and eventually gained independence. But the Jewish Hasmonean family dynasty that emerged from the struggle adopted the style of Hellenistic monarchs, and tensions grew between the dynasty and conservative religious leaders.

Controversial political acts by the Hasmoneans had important bearing on New Testament tensions. One source of tension was the Hasmoneans' conquest and forced conversion to Judaism of the people in the region of the Sea of Galilee; by the first century AD, the area was solidly Jewish, but mistrust remained of its "hillbilly" population. Another notable group was the Samaritans, who occupied the territory between Judea and Galilee. This group emerged after the exile to practice a modified form of Judaism despised by the Jerusalem religious establishment. Ongoing resentment between Jews and Samaritans is assumed in the New Testament, most famously in one of Jesus' parables (Luke 10:29–37).

The Hasmonean period also saw the rise of several Jewish groups influential in the New Testament period. The Pharisees (Greek for "set apart") were offended by Hasmonean Hellenization and strove to return Jews to obedience to the law. They organized *synagogues* (Greek for "assemblies") for worship and instruction and were largely responsible for the development of rabbinic Judaism following the tumultuous events of the first century AD. A second influential group of Jews were the Sadducees, consisting of aristocratic families who produced the high priests and administered the temple. They also conducted whatever military and financial affairs were not managed by the ruling powers, with whom they were closely aligned. They differed with the Pharisees on many religious issues, including rejection as scripture of all the Old Testament other than the Pentateuch, and denial of an afterlife. A third important group, not mentioned in the New Testament, were the Essenes. This group regarded the temple establishment as corrupt and developed separate communities to focus on ritual purity and observance of the law. One of their settlements used nearby caves to hide numerous sacred texts;

these would later become the most important archaeological discovery of modern times, the Dead Sea Scrolls, which the next chapter will describe further.

Roman Conquest

By the mid-first century BC, Rome was on the rise as a world power. In 63 BC, Roman general Pompey marched into Judea with little resistance from the Hasmoneans, who were weakened by their own infighting. The Romans at first appointed a series of local rulers to administer in their name the area roughly corresponding to modern Israel, which eventually became the Roman territory of Judea in its province of Syria. One of the first of those to rule for Rome was Herod, the half-Jewish son of a Hasmonean politician.

Herod took over in 37 BC, married a Hasmonean princess, and later declared himself king of the Jews. He was known as Herod the Great—not because he was popular with the Jews but because he engaged in major building projects, including the renovation of the Jerusalem temple, numerous palaces, and even a coastal city for the Romans' headquarters, Caesarea.

Herod's reputation for cruelty is legendary. Although there is no extra-biblical record of his slaughter of babies in Bethlehem, contemporary accounts record his murder of several of his own sons, wives, and anyone else he suspected of plotting against his reign. When Herod died in 4 BC, the territories that he ruled for Rome were at first divided between his surviving sons, one of whom (Herod Antipas) is mentioned in the Gospels as the killer of John the Baptist. After more political trouble, however, the Romans ruled Judea through procurators, who were essentially tax collectors with a military force. The most famous of these was Pontius Pilate.

Although the Roman headquarters were on the coast, they kept a Jerusalem fortress called the Antonia which looked down over the temple area, and the procurators often rounded up real or potential rebels for public execution by crucifixion, probably on the Mount of Olives above the temple in order to maximize the visibility of their power.

Rebellion and the Reconstitution of Judaism

Judea's restless population had never forgotten how they threw off foreign dominance under the Hasmoneans, and its location on the eastern edge of the Roman Empire made Judea a suspected locus of sedition and revolt. Tensions mounted in the middle decades of the first century AD as a series of incompetent, vindictive procurators clashed with Jews who hoped for independence. When an actual revolt began in AD 66, the Jews' initial success prompted Rome to send an overwhelming army, which moved methodically from north to south, besieged Jerusalem in AD 70, destroyed the city and temple, and cleaned up the last vestiges of resistance by AD 74.

The early Christians did not take part in the revolt against Rome and moved their base of operations away from Jerusalem. The Jews, without the temple as a focal point of religious activity, soon reconstituted Judaism around the study of the Torah. The country, however, remained in turmoil, and another armed rebellion occurred between AD 132–135. This time the Romans under Emperor Hadrian leveled Jerusalem, built a Roman settlement over the ruins named Aelia Capitolina, and barred Jews from the area. Judaism lived on in the diaspora until the twentieth century, when Jews returned to Palestine and re-established nation status in 1948.

Jewish Religion in the New Testament Era

Although the New Testament is written entirely in Greek, it is very much a Jewish book. Jesus and his disciples were Jews for whom Greek was a second or third language after Aramaic and possibly Hebrew. All of the New Testament writings are written by Jews (possibly excepting Luke), and all assume familiarity with the life and literature of first century Judaism. Indeed, the first Christians thought of themselves not as a separate religion but as a movement within Judaism. In order to read the New Testament, and especially the Gospels, intelligently, it is essential to understand something of the rich religious life of the Jews at the time of Jesus.

The primary institution of Judaism at the time of Jesus was the *temple*. The original structure built by Solomon in the tenth century BC was destroyed by the Babylonians in 587 BC, rebuilt about 515 BC, and completely renovated by Herod beginning about 20 BC. The temple was destroyed in the First Jewish War in AD 70, ending the so-called Second Temple Period. All that remains of the temple of Jesus' day is a part of the enormous wall which supported the western part of the platform upon which the temple was built, known today as the Wailing Wall. At the time of Jesus, the work was still progressing on the twenty-six acre site. When finished, the structure was faced with white marble and trimmed with gold. Visible from a distance, and especially impressive looking down from the eastern approach atop the Mount of Olives, the temple was the centerpiece of Jewish culture.

The temple was far more than an architectural wonder. Its primary function was to serve as the location for sacrifices, which could only occur on this site. The regulations for the system are laid down in the Old Testament Law. The idea behind the system is to remind the people that, because of man's sinfulness, the maintenance of a right relationship to God is costly. Life must be given: animals, plants, and the devotion of God's people. A balanced and ordered system involved three basic activities:

> Daily public sacrifices occurred at the altar on the east side of the temple on behalf of Jews everywhere.
>
> Twice a day, at dawn and in the late afternoon, priests killed and burnt a year-old lamb, made offerings (usually of grain), recited the *Shema* (a prayer consisting in part of Deut 6:4–9), carried incense through the main room of the temple, and sang psalms.
>
> Private sacrifices, either to offer thanksgiving or to make peace with God, were made by Jews with the assistance of the priests. For example, in the case of an animal sacrifice for sin, a worshiper would bring the animal into the Court of Men, where it would be killed. The blood and fat were poured out on the altar fire, and the meat was eaten by the priests.

The Jews celebrated six annual festivals, where additional offerings and ceremonies took place. Jews made pilgrimages from all over the Roman world for these holy days, sometimes doubling the population of Jerusalem. The most important of these were Passover, commemorating the Exodus from Egypt (March-April), and the Day of Atonement or Yom Kippur (mid-September).

It is important to recognize the significance of the synagogue in the New Testament period. Although Jews all over the Roman world centered their attention, even from a distance, on the events taking place in the temple, the synagogue might be regarded as a critical supplement to the religious diet. Pharisees developed synagogues in the intertestamental period, probably at first in homes or tents. By the New Testament era, the gatherings took place in dedicated buildings that took on the name, just as the Christian "church," originally a reference to people, later became associated with a structure. Synagogues served a variety of purposes: assembly, worship, scripture reading and teaching, prayer, and education. The synagogue was never intended to compete with the temple; however, when the temple was destroyed, the synagogue system was an obvious way to facilitate the survival of Judaism, with a focus on obedience to the law under the leadership of a rabbi (Hebrew for "my master"). Rabbinic Judaism came to understand the older system of sacrifice and temple ritual as ongoing in a spiritual sense, and the festivals were continued in the belief that God recognizes devotion apart from the actual temple rituals. The synagogue was also important to the early expansion of Christianity. As long as the new faith was considered a form of Judaism, a religion tolerated by the empire, Christians were allowed to gather without violating the Roman law against assembly.

For Further Study:

1. How is Alexander's conquest like or unlike the rise of America in the 20th century in terms of cultural impact? Do American values contribute to or conflict with biblical standards of morality?

2. From the intertestamental period, choose either a major historical event (Alexander's conquest, rise of the Hasmoneans, Roman conquest, destruction of the temple), one of the Jewish sects (Sadducees, Pharisees, Essenes), or an aspect of Jewish religion (temple, feasts, synagogue), and do further research in relation to New Testament issues, especially the clash with Hellenism.

3. Research the transformation from temple-centered worship to rabbinic Judaism, and consider how this change affected Judaism in relation to early Christianity.

4. Research everyday life and belief for either pagans or Jews in the first century AD. How comfortably or safely did most people live? Do we know how important religion was to them, or how open they were to new ideas?

Chapter 14

Old Testament Plus

The period from the close of the Hebrew canon to the first century AD was a prolific period of Jewish writing. Although much of this intertestamental literature is lost, enough survives to exceed the word count of the entire Bible. We will consider this large body of material by category.

The Old Testament

By the time of Jesus, the Old Testament came in three "flavors." The Hebrew version was essentially the same as the text upon which our English translations are based, with the books in slightly different order. Since the common language in Palestine at the time of Jesus was not Hebrew but Aramaic, Jewish scholars composed a series of loose translations into this language, known as the *Targums*. Outside of Palestine, many Jews spoke only Greek, so Jews in Alexandria, Egypt, created a translation beginning in the second century BC that became known as the *Septuagint* or *LXX* (Greek: "seventy," for the number of translators). The Septuagint is very important for New Testament studies because it was the Bible of the early Christians, and most of the quotations of the Old Testament in the New Testament are taken directly from the LXX.

Apocrypha

A group of writings commonly labeled the *Apocrypha* (Greek: "hidden things") were excluded from the canon by the Jews in Palestine but included by other Jews, including those who produced the Septuagint. The early Christian scholar Jerome translated the Apocrypha into common Latin (the Vulgate) along with the rest of the Old Testament. Although Jerome did not regard these writings as scripture, his Latin translation, which included the Apocrypha, became the standard Bible of the Church. In the sixteenth century, Protestant reformers excluded the Apocrypha because these writings were not regarded as canonical by the Jews and because they were not important to New Testament writers. In response, the Roman Catholic Church officially recognized the Apocrypha with the status *deuterocanonical* ("second canon") and continues to regard them as scripture, although in practice they are given less attention than the rest of the canon. This explanation is further complicated by the fact that Greek Orthodox and Slavonic branches of Christianity include a few additional writings from this period; all are included in the NRSV with notes in the table of contents to explain the distinctions. Below are the books of the Apocrypha grouped by subject matter, with those accepted by Roman Catholics in *italics*:

> History: *Additions to Esther, 1–2 Maccabees,* 3–4 Maccabees, 1 Esdras
> Prophecy: *Baruch*
> Moralizing Fiction: *Tobit, Judith, Susanna, Bel and the Dragon*
> Wisdom: *Wisdom of Solomon, Ecclesiasticus*
> Devotional Poetry: Prayer of Manasseh, *Prayer of Azariah and the Song of the Three Young Men,* Psalm 151
> Epistle: *Letter of Jeremiah*
> Apocalyptic: 2 Esdras

These books, written in the second and first centuries BC, enrich our understanding of the history and religious life of the Jews during this period. The historical books of 1–2 Maccabees are primary sources for the early Hasmonean period, and imaginative works like Judith and Bel and the Dragon give us insight into creative attempts of Jews to encourage faith. We are also indebted to the books of Tobit, The Wisdom of Solomon, and Ecclesiasticus (also called The Wisdom of Jesus ben Sirach) for insight into the personal piety of the Jews at the time and the ways in which they worked out their struggle with Hellenism.

Consider this excerpt from the book of Ecclesiasticus (14–15, NRSV), written by an upper class Jew of the second century BC. In style, the book is patterned after the Old Testament book of Proverbs. The content, however, is clearly influenced by Hellenism:

> My son, treat yourself well, if you can afford it,
> and present worthy offerings to the Lord.
> Remember that death will not delay,
> and the decree of Hades [the Greek realm of the dead] has not been shown to you.
> Do good to a friend before you die,
> and reach out and give to him as much as you can.
> Do not deprive yourself of a happy day;
> let not your share of desired good pass by you.
> Will you leave the fruit of your labors to another,
> and what you acquired by toil to be divided by lot?
> Give, and take, and amuse yourself,
> because in Hades one cannot look for luxury.
> All living beings become old like a garment,
> for the decree from of old is,
> You must surely die!
> Blessed is the man who meditates on wisdom
> and who reasons intelligently.
> He who reflects in his mind on her ways
> will also ponder her secrets. . . .

Pseudepigrapha

Miscellaneous Jewish writings of the period 200 BC–AD 200 are collected under the title *Pseudepigrapha*. The title means "falsely written" and refers to the tendency of these books to be written under the name of an ideal Old Testament character. The collection is considerably longer than the Old Testament and contains works in several different languages. Additional writings from the Dead Sea Scrolls were produced during this period of time and qualify as the same kind of writing but are usually published and studied separately. Like the books of the Apocrypha, the pseudepigraphal books are extremely important in revealing the thought world of Judaism during this important historical period. Here is a list of some of the most important titles by category:

> *Moralizing Fiction*: Letter of Aristeas, Joseph and Asenath, Testaments of the Twelve Patriarchs, Testament of Job, Testament of Abraham
> *Old Testament Expansion*: Jubilees, Life of Adam and Eve, Pseudo-Philo, Martyrdom and Ascension of Isaiah, Lives of the Prophets
> *Wisdom*: Words of Ahiqar
> *Devotional Poetry*: Psalms of Solomon, Odes of Solomon
> *Apocalyptic*: 1–2 Enoch, Sybilline Oracles, 4 Ezra, 2 Baruch or Apocalypse of Baruch

As in the Apocrypha, the dominant issue in these writings is the struggle of the Jews with Hellenism. The tale of Joseph and Asenath, for example, is a transparent attempt to marry (literally) the two cultures in a way that allows Judaism to triumph—but in a form that differs in many respects from that portrayed in the Old Testament. Here an Egyptian princess falls in love with the biblical Joseph, but he stands aloof until she repents and converts to Judaism:

> And as Asenath went up to kiss Joseph, Joseph stretched out his right hand and put it on her chest between her two breasts, and her breasts were already standing upright like handsome apples. And Joseph said, "It is not fitting for a man who worships God . . . to kiss a strange woman who will bless with her mouth dead and dumb idols and eat from their table bread of strangulation and drink from their libation a cup of insidiousness and anoint herself with ointment of destruction. (JosAsen 8)

Asenath responds to these seductive words by renouncing her pagan ways and repenting in a pile of ashes for seven days, after which Joseph accepts her. The story continues:

> And Joseph put his arms around her, and Asenath put hers around Joseph, and they kissed each other for a long time and both came to life in their spirit. And Joseph kissed Asenath and gave her spirit of life, and he kissed her the second time and gave her spirit of wisdom, and he kissed her the third time and gave her spirit of truth . . . . . And her father and mother and his whole family came from the field which as their inheritance. And they saw Asenath like the appearance of light, and her beauty was like heavenly beauty. And they saw her sitting with Joseph and dressed in a wedding garment. And they were amazed at her beauty and gave glory to God who gives life to the dead. And after this they ate and drank and celebrated. (JosAsen 19–20)

Old Testament Plus
Apocalyptic Literature

The rise of *apocalyptic* literature during the intertestamental period has an important bearing on New Testament ideas, including the entire book of Revelation, which we will consider in a later chapter. This kind of writing contains certain common features indicative of Jewish hopes for the future. Chief among these features is the notion that God will soon break into history to reverse the power structures; that is, to destroy his enemies and set up a kingdom for his chosen people with a leader descended from King David. Such desires were fueled by the Jews' insignificance on the world scene. Dominated by a succession of foreign powers that did not honor their God, and appalled by the impurity of the Hasmonean family and the Sadducees, Jews longed for a leader who would reward them for their righteousness. In apocalyptic writing, this will occur as the culmination of an end-of-time cosmic struggle between the forces of evil and good. The *eschaton* (Greek for "end of time") is typically described in a series of visions of the future or levels of heaven. Apocalyptic writers rarely, if ever, convey the call to higher morality typical of Old Testament prophetic books; rather, they assume the righteousness of the group with which they identify. The writers are typically pseudonymous, taking the name of an important figure from Israel's past.

The example of apocalyptic writing below is from the Dead Sea Scrolls, which were probably produced by the Essene sect. This group anticipated ruling the world with the aid of two human messiahs (one priestly, one kingly) as a reward for their faithfulness to God's Law. The eagerness to enter into this dominion led the Essenes to ally themselves with rebel forces in the Jewish war of AD 66–74, during which the Romans destroyed their community—but not before they concealed their precious scrolls in cliffside caves at Qumran, where they lay hidden for 1900 years. The scrolls contains fragments of nearly every Old Testament books, a thousand years older than the next-oldest manuscripts, and generally affirm the remarkable accuracy of the Jews in transcribing their scriptures by hand over many centuries. The scrolls also contain both familiar and previously unknown literary works that shed much light on Jewish beliefs in the first century BC and first century AD. The following excerpt from the War Rule, first discovered at Qumran, exemplifies apocalyptic hope at that time:

> This shall be a time of salvation for the people of God, an age of dominion for all the members of His company, and of everlasting destruction for all the company of Satan. The confusion of the sons of Japheth [code for Rome] shall be great and Assyria [Rome] shall fall unsuccoured. The dominion of the Kittim [Gentiles] shall come to an end and iniquity shall be vanquished, leaving no remnant; for the sons of darkness, there shall be no escape.

> Rise up, O Hero!
> Lead off Thy captives, O Glorious One!
> Gather up Thy spoils, O Author of mighty deeds!
> Lay Thy hand on the neck of Thine enemies
> and Thy feet on the pile of the slain!
> Smite the nations, Thine adversaries,
> and devour flesh with Thy sword!
> Fill Thy land with glory

and Thine inheritance with blessing!
Let there be a multitude of cattle in Thy fields,
and in Thy palaces
silver and gold and precious stones!
O Zion, rejoice greatly!
Rejoice all you cities of Judah!
Keep your gates ever open
that the hosts of the nations
may be brought in!
Their kings shall serve you
and all your oppressors shall bow down before you;
they shall lick the dust of your feet. (1QM 1, 12)

The next passage, from the second-to-first century BC book of 1 Enoch, is not only typical of apocalyptic but also helpful in understanding the tension in the Gospels between the Jewish hope for a messiah who would be a military deliverer and Jesus' understanding of his own messianic role. In this passage, the messiah is called Son of Man, and he may be (there is some debate) not only a human king but also a divine being who exists with God before his earthly reign:

And in that place I saw the fountain of righteousness
Which was inexhaustible: and around it were many fountains of wisdom:
And all the thirsty drank of them, and were filled with wisdom,
And their dwellings were with the righteous and holy and elect.
And at that hour that Son of man was named
In the presence of the Lord of Spirits, . . .
All who dwell on the earth shall fall down and worship him, . . .
In these days downcast in countenance shall the kings of the earth become,
And the strong who possess the land because of the works of their hands,
For on the day of their anguish and affliction they shall not be able to save themselves.
And I will give them over into the hands of mine elect: . . .
For they have denied the Lord of Spirits and his Anointed [messiah]. . . .
And he caused the sinners to pass away and be destroyed from off the face of the earth,
And those who have led the world astray, with chains shall they be bound,
And in their assemblage-place of destruction shall they be imprisoned,
And all their works vanish from the face of the earth . . . .
And the word of that Son of man shall go forth . . .
And all shall walk in his ways since righteousness never forsaketh him:
With him will be their dwelling-places, and with him their heritage,
And they shall not be separated from him for ever and ever and ever.
And so there shall be length of days with that Son of man,
And the righteous shall have peace and an upright way
In the name of the Lord of Spirits for ever and ever.

Acknowledgments:

Excerpts above from the pseudepigrapha are quoted from Charlesworth, James H., *The Old Testament Pseudepigrapha*. 2 vols. New York: Doubleday, 1985. This text provides ample introductions and notes for the collection. The translation of the Qumran War Rule is by Vermes, Geza, *The Dead Sea Scrolls in English*. 3rd ed. New York: Viking Penguin, 1987.

For Further Study:

1. Choosing any category of writing that you have already studied in this text, read portions of the same from the apocrypha or pseudepigrapha and comment on similarities and differences, with particular focus on the struggle with Hellenism.

2. How would you explain the popularity of apocalyptic literature from an historical and psychological perspective? Do you regard this explanation as complete?

3. Research the importance of the discovery of the Dead Sea Scrolls, both in terms of previously undiscovered texts and preservation of the Old Testament.

4. Does the truth/Truth distinction considered earlier in this text make it possible to include the apocryphal/pseudepigraphical writings as "sacred texts" or "Scripture," or must the canon be established by religious authorities (perhaps under God's direction)? For the person of faith, is it necessary to believe in both the inspiration of the books and the inspiration of the process of choosing them?

Section Five

Gospel and the Life and Teachings of Jesus

Chapter 15

One Story, Four Versions

What is a Gospel and Why Do We Have Them?

The word *gospel* is from the Anglo-Saxon *godspell*, which is a literal translation of the Latin *evangelium*, and Greek *euangelion,* meaning "good news." We capitalize *Gospel* when referring to the book (as in "read the Gospels"), and we use the lower case *gospel* when referring to the message (as in "preach the gospel"). Obviously the word "evangelist" also comes from the same word; we capitalize *Evangelist* when referring to one of the four authors Matthew, Mark, Luke, and John.

There is nothing else quite like the Gospels that came before them, so the term is difficult to define in terms of literary type or genre. The Gospels are not biography in the modern sense, because they only cover a short period of the life of Jesus, and even that selectively. Even more importantly, each is carefully crafted to stress particular themes. So a better definition might be this: a Gospel is a detailed written expression of a particular concept of the career of Jesus and its meaning. This expression involves both a presentation of the identity of the main character and some guidance for behavior and belief on the part of his followers.

Why write the Gospels in the first place? Many early Christians, perhaps even leaders like Paul, knew the basic message of Jesus and a few details about his life and teachings but lacked the fuller story. As the first generation of believers began to die off, it made sense to write down and combine information from eyewitness accounts, interviews, or personal memory. Once the first writer did this (almost certainly Mark), the other three writers, who had additional material to include or other themes to stress, produced three more Gospels. The differences between them were recognized immediately, but leaders rejected a single, harmonized account in favor of four diverse documents, each with distinctive emphases. From a literary perspective, this was a good call, because each is a masterfully written document deserving independent consideration.

In this chapter, you will learn about the relationships between the Gospels and the distinctive features of each. In the following chapter, you will read and respond to portions of one, the Gospel of Matthew.

Synoptic Relationships

Even a quick reading reveals that the Gospels of Matthew, Mark, and Luke are very much alike and yet also present important differences. The attempt to understand this is called the *Synoptic problem* (*synoptic*, Greek for "seen together"). Proposed explanations for the relationships between the Synoptic Gospels take into account the following facts:

1. When detailed agreement occurs between any two of the three Synoptics, one of the two is almost always Mark.
2. Most of Mark (95 percent) appears in either Matthew or Luke.
3. Matthew and Luke share some material (25 percent) which does not appear in Mark.
4. The sequence of events tends to follow Mark; that is, the other two never agree with each other against Mark in terms of the order of events.

The result, proposed by scholars known as *source critics*, is called the *Mark-Q documentary hypothesis*. This suggests simply that Mark wrote first, and that later (probably independent of one another), Matthew and Luke incorporated most of Mark along with a second, hypothetical source, which scholars refer to as Q (for the German word *Quelle*: "source"). The Q material consists primarily of sayings of Jesus which were probably collected and written down by about AD 50. Matthew and Luke appear to choose, re-arrange, and alter this material quite freely, but they follow Mark's general order of events. It is also interesting to note that when they incorporate material from Mark, the passages (scholars call them *pericopes*) are almost always shortened or "streamlined" by Matthew and Luke. So although Mark is much shorter, the stories it contains are actually longer. Some scholars believe that Matthew and Luke had additional written sources (designated M and L, respectively), which account for the remaining material unique to each—most of which is in their first few chapters.

The Mark-Q documentary hypothesis has gained almost universal acceptance among scholars. It does not, of course, account for the Gospel of John, which shares with the other three only some major events in the public career of Jesus. It is not known if John was written with knowledge of the Synoptics and a desire to supplement them or if the author worked independently. In any case, the resulting four Gospels are each remarkable documents, revolutionary both in terms of creativity and impact. We will now consider the distinctive features of each in their probable chronological order. The section on each Gospel will introduce each Gospel's purpose, author, circumstances of writing, and characteristics.

The Gospel According to Mark

Mark's purpose is to reveal the triumph of the Cross. This statement is deceptively simple. Behind it is Mark's creation of a kind of literature that as far as we know was unique to that point in history: a complex construction which informs, preaches, and responds to its audience all at the same time.

On the simplest level, Mark writes something like a biography, informing its audience with the "facts of the case" concerning Jesus. On another level, it is a sermon, undoubtedly meant to be read out loud, since few people were literate at the time. It offers Christian doctrine and instruction about living, complete with the appropriate "audience response" written into narrative sections (e.g., "they all wondered"). But perhaps at the most intriguing level, Mark's Gospel is a response to the scandal of

Jesus' death. In the Roman world at the time, suffering was to be avoided, pleasure to be cultivated. How could the Christian message be true when its followers experienced the pain of persecution and its very founder had died a shameful death? Mark's response is not to hide the suffering of Jesus but to do just the opposite: to show that it was all part of God's plan, anticipated by Jesus himself, revealed little by little, and performed triumphantly. Indeed, Mark devotes so much space (about one-third of the Gospel) to the story of Jesus' final days that his Gospel has been called "a Passion story with a preface." In the choices that he makes concerning organization and content, then, Mark constructs an extended argument that the Cross is not shameful, but truly good news.

The Gospel of Mark does not contain its author's name, but early and reliable tradition associates it with John Mark, an associate of Paul, Peter, and other apostles. The tradition maintains that in his Gospel, Mark accurately records the reminiscences of Peter, possibly while both were residing in Rome in the middle of the first century AD. The general purpose outlined above, along with his occasional definitions of Aramaic terms and his introduction of Latin terms, suggests that Mark wrote for a gentile audience, most likely the Christian church in Rome. Most scholars regard the range for date of writing as AD 60–70.

The structure of Mark's Gospel is a straightforward sequence of events beginning not with Jesus' birth but with the beginning of his public ministry. It ends with a brief and abrupt reference to Jesus' resurrection, leading many scholars to speculate that, soon after it was written, the original ending was lost and a paragraph or two added.

Mark is often characterized as the Gospel of action. The narrative moves quickly, with stories linked together simply by the words "and" or "immediately." Except for the instruction about discipleship in chapter 10, Jesus does not stop to teach. Compared to the other Gospels, we might regard Mark as a graphic novel: a series of images of Jesus in action that move the reader quickly and directly to the climax. The vocabulary and writing style are popular and simple, not literary by the standards of the time.

Drama is another term often applied to Mark. The Gospel contains many elements of the Greek dramas which were as much a part of life in the gentile world as films are today. The succession of scenes dominated by dialogue, the comedic twist of the resurrection after the tragedy setup of the crucifixion, and even the prologue-act-epilogue structure contribute to this theatrical impression.

Another literary feature which stands out in Mark is the gradual disclosure of Jesus. In the early chapters, clues as to the true significance and purpose of Jesus are laid between the lines. Miracles are not explained, parables are explained only to the disciples, and Jesus often commands secrecy after he heals. Some scholars refer to this gradual revelation as the *Messianic Secret*. Later in the story, we begin to see explicit identification of Jesus as the messiah, and his identity becomes a point of controversy. In the final comedic twist, the culminating pronouncement is made by a soldier at the foot of the cross: "Surely this man was God's Son!" (15:39). The centurion probably meant this in the sense that Jesus was a "divine man" or "hero" in the Roman sense, like the legendary Hercules. But Mark understands that the centurion is also unwittingly affirming the Christian understanding of the title, first announced in the opening sentence of the Gospel. It is also significant that this little proclamation of the gospel at the critical moment is made by a gentile: At the very moment of Jesus' death, the message begins to move out from its origins in Judaism to the wider world.

The Gospel According to Matthew

Matthew's purpose is to demonstrate that Jesus is the Messiah who fulfills the Old Testament. As in the case of Mark, there is evidence here that the author is going far beyond biography to *persuade*. Matthew's Gospel adapts much of Mark to suit the particular needs of his audience, and he weaves in material from Q and from additional sources. The text is infused with Old Testament quotations that show Jesus as the Jewish messiah, including the common formula, "This was done to fulfill what was spoken in the prophet." But by fulfilling the Old Testament, Matthew means more than fulfillment of predictions and types, more even than ending the sacrifice system by Jesus' death. Matthew portrays Jesus as a sort of new Moses who gives instructions about living to his disciples, thereby redefining and intensifying the entire idea of the Jewish Law.

As in the case of Mark, there is no mention of the author in the Gospel of Matthew, whose name was attached to the book by early Christians. Indications from the book itself suggest that Matthew was writing for Greek-speaking Jewish converts to Christianity who could benefit from a demonstration of Jesus' role as messiah and from detailed instruction about living with other Christians. The range of dates for Matthew's composition is AD 65–80.

While following Mark's basic chronology, Matthew arranges Q material and information from other sources in a very orderly manner. The most important instance of this is the arrangement of Jesus' teaching material in five distinct sections called *discourses* (ch 5–7, 9–11, 13, 18, 23–25), each of which concludes with a similar summary linking it to the subsequent narrative. This fivefold division may in fact reflect Matthew's portrayal of Jesus as a new Moses, with this new "law" corresponding to the Pentateuch.

Despite the fact that this Gospel is almost twice the length of Mark, Matthew streamlines the individual stories taken from Mark, eliminating unnecessary words and modifying expressions for clarity. The fast-paced style of Mark gives way here to a more measured approach consistent with the long pauses for discourse material.

The Gospel According to Luke

Luke's purpose is to compose an orderly account of the truth about Jesus. This statement borrows heavily from Luke's own terminology, since he is the only Evangelist who introduces his book with his own statement of purpose:

> Since many have undertaken to set down an orderly account of the events that have been fulfilled among us, just as they were handed on to us by those who from the beginning were eyewitnesses and servants of the word, I too decided, after investigating everything carefully from the very first, to write an orderly account for you, most excellent Theophilus, so that you may know the truth concerning the things about which you have been instructed. (1:1–4)

Luke's repetition of the word "orderly" does not imply that Mark or Matthew are somehow disorderly: Luke follows Mark meticulously and is probably not aware of Matthew's existence. Rather, he wishes to collate material from several sources—Mark, Q, and others at his disposal—in an effective sequence for the sake of readers like Theophilus, who may be a sponsor of Luke's work. Luke does not simply string together sources; close scrutiny reveals careful selection and editing of his source material to stress certain themes.

Luke's name is not attached to the Gospel, but we know that the same author wrote the Gospel and Acts, and Luke's name was attached by early tradition that there is no compelling reason to doubt. Luke was a traveling companion of the apostle Paul and probably a Greek-speaking Jew born outside Palestine. The Greek name of Theophilus, the themes of the work, and the fact that Luke is in Rome with Paul at the close of Acts, all point to gentiles as his intended audience. The date range for composition is similar to that for Matthew, AD 65–80.

Luke's Gospel is the longest book in the New Testament and includes the most information among the Gospels concerning Jesus' birth, his teaching about discipleship, and his resurrection. The most distinctive literary feature of Luke's organization is the incorporation of much of Jesus' teaching material into a "road to Jerusalem" travel narrative, which in Mark and Matthew occupies only one chapter. In Luke, however, this material occupies ten chapters (9:51—19:27). The effect of this arrangement is to view the ministry of Jesus as first directed toward a demonstration of his identity as messiah, then toward the preparation of his followers to carry on his ministry. This structure conveys Luke's interest in the story's progression over the two volumes from Galilee to Jerusalem, then (in Acts) from Jerusalem throughout the world and on to Rome. Apart from this, Luke follows the framework of events established by Mark.

Luke shares Matthew's tendency to streamline Mark's material, shortening and modifying passages in order to increase clarity. But unlike Matthew, who stops for discourses, Luke retains Mark's sense of movement without retaining Mark's fast-paced style of writing. Luke accomplishes this by his structuring to give the Gospel a sense of forward momentum. From 9:51, when Jesus "set his face to go to Jerusalem," there is a strong sense of direction. The Gospel ends on this note with the disciples experiencing "great joy" and "blessing God" (24:52), ready for the sequel, the book of Acts.

Universality is another strong theme in Luke. As in the case of Matthew, there is a strong interest in gentiles. But in Luke, it might be argued that the gentiles are only one dimension of the universality of the gospel, which extends more generally to all who are *outsiders* or *outcasts*. From the Jewish perspective, the gentiles fit in this category, and a Gospel which is addressed to them naturally stresses their inclusion in God's plan. But they are not the only kind of outcast stressed by Luke. Women have a more important role in this Gospel than in any of the others (e.g., 1:5–56; 2:36–38; 8:1–3; 24:10–11). Children, similarly, receive greater attention than in the other Gospels (7:12; 8:42; 9:38). The poor, both in terms of financial and physical limitations, are also given special attention by Luke (4:17–19; 14:7–24; 16:19–31). Conversely, the rich are viewed very negatively (14:1–24; 16:1–15). Finally, while "tax collectors and sinners" receive the attention of Jesus in Mark and Matthew, it is Luke who culminates the long teaching section in the famous announcement of salvation for Zacchaeus—no less than a supervisor of tax collectors. The concluding line of this account summarizes the universality theme in Luke: "For the Son of man came to seek and to save the lost" (19:10).

One other peculiar emphasis in Luke worthy of mention is his interest in the dangers of wealth. Much of chapters 6, 12, 14, and 16–19 are taken up with this theme. Although some of this material is contained in Mark and Matthew, Luke includes all of the relevant passages, intensifies the language, and adds other material. In fact, his long travel narrative culminates in the contrast between the rich young ruler who refuses to part with his possessions when confronted by Jesus, and the tax collector Zacchaeus, who gives away half his possessions to the poor immediately and keeps the rest only to repay those he has defrauded.

The Gospel According to John

John's purpose is to urge belief in Jesus as the Son of God who gives eternal life. As in the case of Luke, we are able to borrow terms from the writer's own statement of purpose, which in this case occurs near the end of the book: "These [things] are written so that you may come to believe that Jesus is the Messiah, the Son of God, and that through believing you may have life in his name" (20:31). John's purpose, then, is clearly evangelistic. It is not clear whether he intends the work to be read directly by unbelievers or by believers who will draw from it in their own evangelistic efforts, or both. There is little interest here in specific instruction about discipleship, as in the Synoptics. Instead, the clear focus is on who Jesus is ("the Messiah, the Son of God") and what that truth implies ("that through believing you may have life").

There is no explicit reference in the Gospel to identify its writer, but early tradition names John, one of Jesus' followers, as the author. Many modern scholars dispute this attribution, but most agree that John was the last Gospel written, between AD 80–100.

Like Matthew, John interrupts the narrative with long discourses by Jesus on various topics. The result of these changes is that John's "drama" lacks the journey motif and reads instead as a series of scenes which serve as introductions for extended speeches by the leading actor. Such features, along with the extended prologue (1:1–18) and brief epilogue (21:24–25), may reveal the influence of Greek drama on the Gospel.

John's supplementation of the Synoptics with new material involves not only the narratives and discourses themselves but also the emphases and vocabulary contained in them. One dominant characteristic, implied by the statement of purpose, is the notion of belief in Jesus. Whereas the other Gospels stress "following," a concept which lends itself well to the life of discipleship, John's emphasis on "believing" better serves his evangelistic purpose. Beginning with the highly literary and poetic prologue, and continuing with numerous "I am" statements by Jesus and seven signs performed by him, the fourth Gospel shows great interest in the divinity of Jesus and his central significance for salvation.

John's perspective on the future of the believer differs from the Synoptics in its stress on salvation as a present reality. This is not to deny the afterlife but to stress the present as the time to live as a believer. Some other distinctive features of content are worthy of note. John's Gospel focuses on love for God and for other believers as the primary responsibility of those who believe. The stress in the Synoptics on the *kingdom* gives way here to the term *eternal life*. Numerous contrasts—light vs. darkness, true vs. false, being of God vs. being of the world, etc.—link John's Gospel closely to the Old Testament imagery. Finally, whereas in the Synoptics, Jesus is almost invariably called "the Son of man," in John he is almost invariably "the Son of God" or simply "the Son." This is probably a change of clarification intended to highlight the divinity of Jesus for a Hellenistic audience.

ONE STORY, FOUR VERSIONS

Summary of Gospel Comparisons

You can now begin to appreciate why the early church rejected attempts in the late second century to collate the four Gospels into one. Each has such a distinct perspective that the Church wisely decided to reject the concept of *The* Gospel and retain the concept of the Gospel *According To*. This creates problems—especially the resolution of conflicts in detail between the accounts—and yet in fundamental ways, the four are generally unified in basic chronology, key events, and essential theology. More importantly, the main character is clearly the same person whose compelling personality jumps off the page. He is a worker of miracles who suppresses publicity, a teacher about his own significance who preaches humility, a proclaimer of urgent truth who speaks in riddles, a preacher about forgiveness whose radical demands for behavior defy compliance, a lead actor who marches inexorably toward tragedy and then emerges in surprising triumph. As story, this is compelling, and compellingly presented. Further, each of these four distinct dramas records the response from the audience, which by implication extends from the eyewitnesses on the stage itself, to the original recipients of the Gospels, and to readers ever since. Whether you consider the Gospels tragedy, comedy, or fairy tale, they are literary masterpieces and worthy of closer inspection—to which we turn in the next chapter.

For Further Study:

1. Read the birth narratives in Matthew 1–2 and Luke 1–2, and describe how each conveys the themes described here for each Gospel.

2. Read an early narrative section from one of the Gospels (Mark 1–3, Luke 7–9, or John 1–4) and compare it to an Old Testament narratives in terms of technique. How does the portrayal of Jesus differ from that of an Old Testament hero?

3. Compare Matthew's version of the Beatitudes (blessings), 5:3–12, with that of Luke, 6:20–26. How do the organization and wording lead interpreters to consider Matthew's version more "spiritual" and Luke's more "political"? How are both versions linked to the Old Testament prophets?

4. Examine in detail an account that occurs in all three of the Synoptics and comment on how Matthew and Luke "streamline" Mark's account (e.g., stilling the storm, Matt 8:23–27 / Mark 4:35–41 / Luke 8:22–25; healing Matt 9:18–26 / Mark 5:21–43 / Luke 8:40–66).

5. Research reasons that John's Gospel differs from the Synoptics, and discuss whether these are better explained by different sources, different purposes, or some other reason.

6. Research differences in the accounts of Jesus' resurrection, and discuss whether these are more likely the result of different sources or different themes chosen by each writer.

7. Watch one or more films about the life of Jesus (e.g., *King of Kings, Godspell, Jesus Christ Superstar, Passion of the Christ*) and discuss how each film reflects themes appropriate to its time and intended audience. What are the implications for the creation of the original Gospels? How does film narrative compare to written narrative in terms of effective storytelling?

Chapter 16

Jesus According to Matthew

In order to enable you to appreciate the unity and flow of narrative, we will read through one Gospel in its entirety, stopping here and there to consider more closely Matthew's distinctive themes and narrative techniques. We will also pause to introduce a method of study that will allow you to reach insights into biblical texts with essentially the same methods that scholars use. The one glaring absence in our treatment of Matthew is attention to the parables of Jesus, which the next section of the book will consider in detail.

The Birth of Jesus

The genealogy of Jesus which begins Matthew's Gospel is seldom read carefully, but it contains a rich deposit of material indicative of Matthew's literary technique. The very existence of the genealogy and its placement at the beginning of the Gospel introduce the strong interest throughout the Gospel in Jesus' fulfillment of the Old Testament. Matthew begins by calling Jesus "the son of David, the son of Abraham." Thus he stresses Jesus' fulfillment of Judaism in general (originating with Abraham) and its specific hope for a messiah (originating with David). Matthew also appears to show an interest in arrangement of material for theological purposes: he omits names from the known list of kings in order to come up with a three-part list of fourteen generations each. Fourteen is a multiple of seven, and threes and sevens are spiritually significant numbers in Hebrew tradition. These and other details of the genealogy reveal Matthew's desire to show that from the beginning, Jesus' story has both historic and symbolic significance.

As you read, you will also begin to see Old Testament quotations, most of which signal Matthew's interest in typological prophecy (chapter 11 above, which includes a discussion of Matt 1:23). For example, in Matt 1:21, Joseph is instructed to name the child "Jesus, for he will save his people from their sins." This is an allusion to Ps 130:8: "He will redeem Israel from all his iniquities." The name Jesus, a Greek spelling of the Hebrew name Joshua, means "God (Yahweh) is salvation." Joshua, of course, was the first great deliverer of God's people in the Old Testament; Matthew sees Jesus as the last.

Except for a brief incident recorded by Luke (2:41–52), the Gospels provide no information about Jesus between his infancy and public ministry. We know that while he was growing up in Nazareth, the nearby cities of Sepphoris and Tiberius were built, providing steady and perhaps lucrative employment for local tradesmen like Joseph and his sons (Jesus had several younger brothers and sisters). Work in

Tiberius, which was located on the west shore of the Sea of Galilee, may also explain the contacts of Jesus with the north shore fisherman of Capernaum who would later become his disciples. The content of Jesus' teaching suggests to some scholars that he was not merely a tradesman but was broadly educated, perhaps in a local synagogue. These few hints about the circumstances of Jesus' upbringing, however, leave many questions unanswered.

Read Matthew 1–2

16a: It is natural to wish for a full biography of Jesus, to know something of his childhood and how he became aware of his own mission. If his early life is omitted by design rather than for lack of information, what purpose might the omission serve in terms of the overall story?

16b: Consider Matthew's storytelling in light of what you learned about narrative technique from Old Testament stories (chapter 5 above). Name and illustrate an aspect of effective narrative that you observe, and suggest how this part of the story may foreshadow an important theme developed later in the Gospel.

The Early Career of Jesus

The next section of Matthew that you will read covers Jesus' ministry up to the turning point described in Matt 16, minus the Sermon on the Mount (ch 5–7), which we will consider next. The stress in this material is on the deeds of Jesus that reveal him as messiah.

John the Baptist figures importantly in this material (3:1–17; 11:2–29; 14:6–12). He was evidently a well-known figure in first-century Palestine, so it was particularly important for the Jewish readers of Matthew's Gospel to understand his relation to Jesus. The bizarre clothing and diet of John are items available in the desert, and as such they signify his independence from human influence, his utter dependence on God. This is a self-conscious patterning after the Old Testament prophet Elijah, who is described identically in 2 Kings 1:8. According to Malachi 3:1 and 4:5, the prophet who precedes the messiah will take the role of Elijah.

John's location is also significant. The wilderness is the place of rebellion and wandering in Israel's history; therefore, by going out to John to express repentance, the people are expressing a willingness to be tested again, this time with positive results. When John administers a "baptism of repentance," therefore, it means not merely feeling remorse but also beginning to live righteously in expectation of salvation soon to come. The origins of the practice of baptism are obscure, but may have originated in ritual Jewish washing for spiritual purification. The form of baptism that John practiced must have been unusual or he would not have been designated "the Baptizer."

As we approach the point in the narrative where Jesus begins to attract followers, it is useful to clarify New Testament terms for people of faith. The Gospels identify the appropriate response to Jesus with the verbs *follow* or *believe*. One who did so is usually called a *disciple* ("learner"), and a member of the primary group of twelve is also known as an *apostle* ("one who is sent"). After the Gospels, the New Testament refers to members of the community of faith most often as *believers* or in the aggregate as *brothers* (including women), the *church* (Greek *ekklesia*: "gathering"), or the *Way*, and the term *apostle* is applied not only to the original Twelve but also to missionaries like Paul and his associates. The term *Christian*, initially a term applied by outsiders (Acts 11:26, 26:28, 1 Pet 4:16), is never used in the New Testament by believers for themselves, but it became common by the end of the first century.

Read Matthew 3–4, 8–16:12

16c: A literary technique built into the Gospels (which were originally read aloud to groups) is the description of responses of people to Jesus, which indicate the appropriate response for the hearers of the stories. After quoting or summarizing, in one sentence each, several reactions of crowds or individuals to the deeds or words of Jesus, what conclusions can you draw concerning the intent of Matthew 4–16?

16d: How would you describe the personality of Jesus, and how does Matthew convey that personality? Provide at least five examples to support your portrait.

Interlude: Finding Reasonable Answers to Good Questions

Even without a scholar's knowledge of the original languages and the historical context, it is possible to ask good questions about a biblical text and to reach a high level of understanding and insight. Before returning to the Gospel of Matthew, you will encounter methods of research that you can perform on your own. Practice with these basic tools will enable you to look more deeply for yourself into the biblical text and many other challenging works of literature. At the very least, you will better understand how scholars interpret an ancient text like the Bible, because they use the very interpretive techniques outlined here.

Meaningful interpretation begins with good questions. Good questions begin with curiosity about meaning. Readers of the Gospels find many reasons to be curious about meanings of particular words, statements, and themes; or about connections between biblical material and current religious belief and practice. For example, some of the statements of Jesus to his followers appear to set an impossibly high standard of behavior. What was Matthew's purpose in including such statements? Was he simply reporting what Jesus said, or did he include such material in order to give moral guidance to readers of his Gospel? Were radical demands, like the renunciation of wealth and family, meant as absolute and permanent standards of behavior? Were they meant only for leaders of the community, or only for a brief period to jumpstart the movement? Can we trust that English translations convey precisely the meaning of key terms? Can we answer such questions for ourselves, or must we get help from scholars?

These are the kinds of issues that lead to good questions. Once we consider a text long enough to discover what we do not know, the next step is to formulate a precise question that includes possible options in order to gain control over our inquiry. We should *not* ask, for example, "What is love?" because the question is so open-ended that we never know when we've answered it. A good question has a specific focus and gives plausible (reasonable) options, usually two, to choose from. So we might ask, "When Jesus says to love one's enemies in Matthew 5:33–34, does 'love' mean to feel affection for them or to treat them with kindness?" Note also that a good question also avoids "trick" answers like "both"; if "both" is a possible answer, set up the question this way: "When Jesus says to love one's enemies in Matthew 5:33–34, does 'love' mean both to feel affection for them and to treat them with kindness, or just one of these?"

Here is another example to help you formulate good questions. A statement by Jesus that bothers many readers is Luke 14:33: "So therefore, none of you can become my disciple if you do not give up all your possessions." Here are several good questions to ask: "Does *disciple* in Luke 14:33 refer only to followers of Jesus during his public ministry or to all followers at all times?" "Does *give up* in Luke 14:33 require a physical or only a spiritual separation from possessions?" "Does *all . . . possessions* in Luke 14:33 refer to property or to the totality of one's life?" The rule can be put in one sentence: a good question has a specific point of reference and presents two reasonable options.

Now, how to answer such a question? When dealing with an ancient text in English translation, we must proceed humbly and tentatively, because there may be slight shades of meaning that don't translate well from one language to the next, or across cultures and time. But there is much that we can do armed with a single tool: a *concordance.* This is a book (or computer program) that lists all the instances of a given word in the work being studied.

Scholars of English literature, for example, might come across an obscure word like "orisons" or a common word like "jealous" in the works of Shakespeare. By using a concordance, they can look carefully at surrounding words or explanations in the passages where the word is used; or they can look at ways the same word used in a number of places. In this way, they can better approximate Shakespeare's meaning. Studying the Bible this way is somewhat more complicated, because there are many authors, writing over centuries, in ancient languages. Even the assumption that God has inspired every biblical word does not imply that all words mean exactly the same thing every time they are used. Where does one begin?

Some read a biblical text and proclaim "what it means to me," but this approach is careless, prone to manipulation, and disrespectful to the original writer. Responsible interpretation looks for the *original author's intent*, a principle that applies equally to the study of Shakespeare, a business textbook, or Matthew. An author conveys intended meaning by units of thought as small as individual words, which we sometimes neglect in our haste to understand sentences or paragraphs. Fortunately, we have tools to help us approach the author's intent. One of the most important is the principle of *contextual proximity*. This expression means, very simply, closeness of environment. The principle at work is that, generally, *evidence about meaning begins in the immediate context and diminishes in importance as one gets further from that context.* In New Testament study, a hierarchy of contextual proximity generally holds true. Interpreters consider the occurrence of a word or concept in this general order:

earlier in the paragraph
later in the paragraph
    earlier in the book
    later in the book
    in another work by the same writer
    in an earlier or contemporary New Testament writer
    in a later New Testament writer
        in contemporary extra-canonical material (Septuagint, Dead Sea Scrolls, apocrypha, pseudepigrapha, contemporary Jewish writers Philo and Josephus)
        in later extra-canonical material (early church leaders, New Testament apocrypha, early translations, rabbinic writings up to the 6th century)
        in the Old Testament (higher priority for study of Gospels)

Most of this is common sense, including the flexibility of the hierarchy at the lower levels, where we might judge similarity of *situation* more "proximal" than similarity of *literature*. When considering the teachings of Jesus, for example, the Old Testament and contemporary Jewish writings are usually more helpful than other New Testament texts. For example, the expression "poor in spirit" was used by the Essenes, and its use in their literature may explain Matt 5:3 better than instances of "poor" or "in spirit" in Paul or even in the Old Testament. When employing these lower levels of the hierarchy, the point is to make a case that one occurrence is closer than another to the thought of the author in question.

Using the example just mentioned, here is the result of research that any college or advanced high school student could perform:

> Question: Does "blessed are the *poor in spirit*" in Matthew 5:3 refer to poverty or humility?
>
> Answer: "Poor in spirit" in Matthew 5:3 refers to humility.
>
> 1. The exact term "poor in spirit" is not used elsewhere in the Bible.
>
> 2. The other characteristics described in Matthew 5:3–12 describe attitudes more than outward circumstances.
>
> 3. A "contrite" or "faint" spirit connotes humility: Ps 51:17, 77:3, 142:3, 143:4, Prov 16:19, 29:23, Isa 57:15, 61:1, 66:2.
>
> 4. The Dead Sea Scrolls include several references to "poor in spirit" indicating a sense of personal inadequacy: 1QM 7.5, 11.10, 14.7, 1QS 4.3, 1QH 18.14–15.
>
> 5. "Poor and needy" commonly connotes humility in the Old Testament: Ps 37:14, 40:17, 74:21, 109:22.
>
> 6. The Dead Sea Scroll references appear similar to "hearts melting" before battle in Josh 2:11, 5:1.
>
> 7. Although the parallel passage in Luke (6:20) appears to denote economic condition, the immediate context and other passages in Luke suggest an intent different intent from Matthew's.

The Teaching of Jesus

Jesus' teaching about how his disciples should live is distributed throughout Matthew, but as the earliest and largest block of material, the section known as the Sermon on the Mount merits close attention. By gathering this material from Q and other sources, Matthew casts Jesus in the role of a new Moses. Jesus does not dismiss the Old Testament; rather, he intensifies it. In one of his strongest statements, he claims that "unless your righteousness exceeds that of the scribes and Pharisees, you will never enter the kingdom of heaven" (5:20). To exceed this standard of righteousness does not mean, however, that one must find more laws to avoid breaking. Instead, "higher righteousness" is shown *positively*, by loving actions; and *inwardly or secretly*, by loving motivation which is seldom observable by other people.

Read Matthew 5–7

16e: The word "blessed" in the famous Beatitudes (5:3–12) is sometimes translated or interpreted as "happy." What argument can you make from the immediate context that this word is appropriate or inappropriate, and that this "blessed" state will be realized in the present or in the future?

16f: What is the formula for contrasts in 5:21–47, how is it introduced and summarized (vv. 13–20, 48), and what does it indicate about Jesus' attitude to the Law?

16g: What is the formula to introduce the series of instructions in 6:1–16, and what principle does it convey regarding behavior?

16h: After reviewing the "interlude" regarding good questions and answers, formulate three questions of your own, one each for Matthew chapters 5, 6, and 7. Preface each question with a brief statement about the importance of the issue raised by the question. Your questions may form the basis for further research or group discussion.

Jesus According to Matthew

The Identity of Jesus

Picking up Matthew's narrative in the middle of chapter 16, we first read a pivotal conversation between Jesus and Peter and the accompanying narrative of the Transfiguration. For the first time, Jesus begins to reveal his immediate and ultimate roles in the salvation process. This part of Matthew's Gospel contains the fourth of five major discourses by Jesus; the focus here is on humility and forgiveness. Next is the story of a rich man who is told to give away his possessions and Jesus' warning about the danger of riches.

An important transition begins at 20:17, when Jesus arrives in Jerusalem for the last week of his life. Statements recorded by Matthew include several parables, predictions by Jesus of his death and resurrection, and his predictions about the end of history. Jesus enters Jerusalem (21:1–12) in a self-consciously messianic manner by riding a gentle donkey (as opposed to a war horse), and Matthew draws attention to this act as a fulfillment of the Old Testament prophecy of Zech 9:9. But the people do not grasp the notion that Jesus comes gently and peacefully. Instead, they greet him by spreading their garments and palm branches on the road before him (21:8); such gestures, especially the palm branches (Jewish national symbols), signified the expectation of military conquest or deliverance from foreign domination. Thus, the scene foreshadows the rejection of Jesus. Two incidents follow immediately as symbolic indications of Jesus' anticipation of rejection. The cleansing of the temple (21:12–13) is not a criticism of unfair business practices so much as a sign of judgment on those Jews who have rejected Jesus' message about true righteousness. The cursing of the fig tree (21:18–22), likewise, signifies condemnation of those who reject Jesus, perhaps in allusion to a passage like Jeremiah 8:13, "When I would gather them, says the Lord, there are no grapes on the vine nor figs on the fig tree; even the leaves are withered, and what I gave them has passed away from them."

In the final major discourse in Matthew (chapters 25–26), Jesus predicts the end of time. Note the central role that Jesus claims for himself in these events.

Read Matthew 16:13—25:46

16i: What are the three titles used for Jesus in this section, who uses each, and how many times? Guided only by the descriptions Jesus gives when he uses the title, what definition can you give of Jesus' favorite self-designation?

16j: What incidents of dramatic irony occur in Matthew's storytelling technique in 19:27—20:34?

16k: Does the content or style of Jesus' teaching in this section differ at all from earlier sections, like the Sermon on the Mount? If so, what is it about the content that better fits the end of Jesus' ministry? If not, what purpose might be served by placing this particular content here?

Death and Resurrection of Jesus

The significance of Jesus' death, predicted several times during his ministry, is the focus of his final meal with the disciples. The setting of the Last Supper is particularly important. The Passover festival was (and is) a time for Jews to look back on God's deliverance of his people and to look forward to ultimate deliverance. In Jesus' day, the festival involved not only the sacrifice of a lamb by each family but also a symbolic meal during which the head of the family would describe the meaning of the occasion to its members. Here, Jesus acts as the head of the "family," but he departs radically with the traditional explanation by describing *himself* as the sacrifice. He alludes several times to the wording of Isa 53:10–11, which describes God's suffering servant as one who will "render himself as a guilt offering," "justify the many," and "(bear) the sin of many." In all of these respects, the Passover setting highlights the theme of Old Testament continuity so strongly portrayed in Matthew's Gospel. Indeed, the account of Jesus' last meal portrays him as the ultimate fulfillment of the Old Testament sacrifice system.

The final two chapters of Matthew describe Jesus' death and resurrection. Our purpose in this text is not to judge the historical reliability of the extraordinary events in this account, or even to analyze the many differences of detail between Matthew's version and those of the other Gospels. Obviously, the issues of truth/Truth here have far-reaching implications. But from a literary perspective, we are interested in how Matthew's narrative works. The reader will recognize, first, that these momentous events are covered in just two chapters. Details are spare and evidently chosen carefully to advance the action, only rarely to comment on it. Still, this brief narrative is packed with Old Testament references and allusions, symbols, significant statements by key characters, and a strong sense of forward movement.

Read Matthew 26–28

16l: Who looks most and least responsible for Jesus' death in this section: Judas, the Jewish leaders, the crowds, the disciples, Pilate, or Jesus himself? Explain your choice.

16m: Read Psalm 22 and list the parallels or allusions in Matthew's crucifixion narrative (27:1–43).

16n: What are three or four major themes of Matthew's Gospel that are summarized by 28:18–20, and what specific terms or phrases establish these?

For Further Study:

The first three questions are "contextual proximity" exercises based on the interlude section.

1. Is Jesus purposely exaggerating in Matt 5:29–30 to make a point, does he renounce retaliation altogether, or does he renounce retaliation only in the context of religious persecution?

2. Do the statements in Matt 6:19–34, taken together, mean that wealth is acceptable after one gives what is due to God, or that God will take care of the basic needs of those who renounce wealth for his sake?

3. Matt 7:1–5 condemns judging but does not define it precisely. If Jesus allows for mutual accountability and estimation of character (18:15–17, 7:15–20) is this passage prohibiting all criticism, criticism for actions of which the critic is guilty, or criticism that involves condemnation?

4. Research the title "Son of man" and discuss its usefulness for and by Jesus in contrast to other possible titles.

5. Examine one or more miracle stories in terms of the principles of effective narrative (chapter 5 in this text).

6. Compare Matthew's account of the crucifixion with that of Mark. What differences do you find that might be attributed to narrative technique, and what do these additions or changes accomplish in terms of the effectiveness of the story?

Section Six

Parable as Invitation to the Kingdom and Discipleship

Chapter 17

Principles of Parables

Why Parables?

Parables (italics), which are metaphors extended sometimes to story length, constitute the most distinctive form of teaching in the Gospels. While Jesus did not invent the form (see e.g., 2 Sam 12:1–4; Isa 5:1–7; Ezek 17:3–10), what is unusual is that he employs it constantly. The parables of Jesus are not pleasant little moral lessons like Aesop's fables but weapons of controversy, shattering the prevalent, comfortable beliefs of Jesus' audience concerning religion and morality. His parables are intensely personal, designed to penetrate the husk of self-satisfaction and the distractions of everyday life. They reach to the hearer's essential self and demand response. Most importantly, by taking the form of succinct stories, they allow the hearer an active part in the hearer's own persuasion. To communicate ideas in a brief narrative, as compared to a list of dogmatic statements or an extended argument, is a mark of respect for the audience, allowing creativity not only on the part of the storyteller but also on the part of the hearer. To encounter parables, one must employ imagination.

Note the similarity of this characterization of parables to that of the patriarchal narratives considered earlier in this text. We could make a case that Old Testament narratives function as parables, or that an entire Gospel—not just particular stories within one—functions as an extended parable. In other words, it is very rare that a Gospel offers direct instruction to the audience of what to believe or what to do. Instead, the significance of Jesus and the appropriate response to him beyond the notion that one should "believe" or "follow" is largely left for the reader to work out.

To observe that parables are Jesus' distinctive and most common form of teaching is not to affirm that the original hearers all grasped his meaning. In fact, in the only extended interpretation of one of his parables by Jesus (Matt 13:3–23 / Mark 4:1–25 / Luke 8:4–15), he states that disciples are likely to understand, while outsiders or opponents will not. This apparently harsh statement may reflect a strategy in Jesus' ministry (the "messianic secret," ch 15 above), or it may suggest simply that characters in parables who make wrong choices represent those who do so in real life. The intent may also be to portray Jesus' prophetic role: like Isaiah, whom he quotes in this passage, Jesus' pronunciation in effect enacts what it observes. Whether or not some such principle is at work in the text, we know from experience that some people are unable or unwilling to derive personal lessons from stories. You have probably heard someone say, "I only read nonfiction, because I want to get information and insight *directly.*" Apart from the question of how *direct* any piece of nonfiction is—free of bias, illustrations, or metaphors?—one hopes that such a self-styled literalist will occasionally derive "information and insight" from works of art, sunsets, and small children.

Characteristics of the Parable Form

The general definition of a parable as extended metaphor needs expansion in its Gospel context. In his book *The Parables of the Kingdom*, biblical scholar C. H. Dodd offers this fuller definition: "At its simplest a parable is a metaphor or simile drawn from nature or common life, arresting the hearer by its vividness or strangeness, and leaving the mind in sufficient doubt about its precise application to tease it into active thought" (5).

How do we know we are reading a parable? In many cases, the actual Greek word *parabole* is used in the Gospels to introduce or summarize an instance of the form. But a third of the parables are distinguished from narratives not by a label but by their style. Because they vary in length from one-liners to full-page narratives, not every parable includes every characteristic of the form. Consideration of the entire collection, however, yields certain recognizable features. Common features of *content* in the parables include the following:

    Defining God's kingdom
    Dangers of wealth
    Condemnation of hypocrisy
    Necessity of forgiveness
    Humility
    Impending judgment of the world or of Jesus' opponents
    Urgent necessity of decision
    God's mercy

Common features of *style* in the parables include the following:

    Introduction with a question or comparative statement ("the kingdom is like . . .")
    Action involving a single event in past time
    Brevity: no extraneous details
    Action is realistic, does not involve fables or miracles
    Direct discourses and monologues, especially internal monologue
    Characters are human, not animal or supernatural beings
    Characters are often upper class or rulers
    Setting is usually rural
    Characters are almost never named
    No personality development: focus on conduct rather than motives
    Key words and phrases are repeated
    One major thought
    Ending involves a compelling summary statement
    Hearer is challenged to make a decision

Principles of Parables

The table below lists the parables found in the Gospels. The careful observer will note some useful features from this table. Of the thirty-seven parables, eight are "triple tradition," occurring in all three Synoptics, which may signal them as particularly important. The five "double tradition" parables are usually associated by scholars with the Q source, because they all appear in Matthew and Luke. Single tradition parables may have come from separate sources known only to Matthew or Luke, or they may have been present in Q but chosen for inclusion by only Matthew or only Luke. One also notes from the list that, true to their respective styles, Matthew tends to group parables within Jesus' major discourses, while Luke tends to cluster them in his central travel narrative, chapters 9–19. In terms of Synoptic relationships and themes, it is also interesting to note that all but one of the parables in Mark are repeated in both Matthew and Luke, and that the parables unique to Matthew tend to focus on the kingdom of God, while Luke's stress the nature of discipleship.

There are no parables in John, but there are three extended allegories with parable-like features: The Bread of Life (6:31–38), the Good Shepherd (10:1–18), the Vine and Branches (15:1–17). Elsewhere in the New Testament there are no parables, but there are extended allegories in Galatians 4 and Hebrews 9.

Gospel Parables by Traditional Title, in Canonical Order

Number and Title	Matthew	Mark	Luke
1 The Growing Seed		4:26–29	
2 The Two Debtors			7:41–43
3 The Lamp under a Bushel	5:14–15	4:21–25	8:16–18
4 The Good Samaritan			10:29–37
5 The Friend at Night			11:5–8
6 The Rich Fool			12:16–18
7 The Wise and Foolish Builders	7:24–27		6:46–49
8 New Wine into Old Wineskins	9:16–17	2:21–22	5:37–39
9 The Strong Man	12:29	3:27	11:21–22
10 The Sower	13:3–23	4:3–15	8:5–15
11 The Wheat and the Weeds	13:24–30		
12 The Barren Fig Tree			13:6–9
13 The Mustard Seed	13:31–32	4:30–32	13:18–19
14 The Leaven	13:33		13:20–21
15 Hidden Treasure	13:44		
16 The Pearl	13:45		
17 Drawing in the Net	13:47–50		
18 The Wedding Feast			14:7–14

19 Counting the Cost			14:28–33
20 The Lost Sheep	18:10–14		15:4–6
21 The Unforgiving Servant	18:23–35		
22 The Lost Coin			15:8–9
23 The Prodigal Son			15:11–32
24 The Unjust Steward			16:1–13
25 The Rich Man and Lazarus			16:19–31
26 The Master and Servant			17:7–10
27 The Unjust Judge			18:1–9
28 The Pharisee and the Tax Collector			18:10–14
29 The Workers in the Vineyard	20:1–16		
30 The Two Sons	21:28–32		
31 The Wicked Tenants	21:33–41	12:1–9	20:9–16
32 The Great Banquet	22:1–14		14:15–24
33 The Budding Fig Tree	24:32–35	13:28–31	12:35–38
34 The Faithful Servant	24:42–51	13:34–37	12:35–48
35 The Ten Virgins	25:1–13		
36 The Talents	25:14–30		19:12–27
37 The Sheep and the Goats	25:31–46		

In the next chapter, we will take a close look at several representative Gospel parables to appreciate in greater depth the technique and impact of this important form.

For Further Study:

1. Research Old Testament parables and compare features of content and style with the Gospels (Judg 9:7–21; 2 Sam 12:1–4; 1 Kings 20:39–42; 2 Kings 14:8–10; Isa 5:1–7; 28:21–29; Ezek 16; 17:1–24; 19:1–14; 20:45–49; 23; 24:3–14)

2. Based on your study of Old Testament narrative and parables, does the book of Jonah appear to be historical narrative or parable?

3. Research parables or similar kinds of writing like Aesop's fables as a basis of comparison to the Gospel parables.

4. Compose a parable of your own in a modern setting, using as many of the features as possible from the list above for Gospel parables.

5. Distinguish between parable, folk or fairy tale, and allegory, with a famous example of each; alternately, compose your own version of the same idea conveyed briefly in each form.

Chapter 18

Parables of Kingdom and Discipleship

As we move toward consideration of individual parables, it is useful to categorize. A glance at the list in the last chapter reveals a variety of length among the parables, from a single verse to a full page. The list also shows clusters of parables, organized early and late in Matthew and in the middle of Luke. What the list does not convey is that these clusters of parables are thematic. Matthew's parables focus on the nature of the kingdom of heaven: that it is coming soon, and that inclusion will not follow the expectations of the religious establishment. Luke's cluster of parables in his travel narrative focus on the nature of discipleship: that it requires humility, forgiveness, and renunciation of wealth. We will consider several short parables from Matthew that portray the kingdom of God, and then a group of longer parables from Luke on the subject of discipleship.

Read Matthew 13

18a: This chapter opens with the important triple tradition Parable of the Sower, which is accompanied by an explanation. Following that, Matthew includes six more short parables on the kingdom, all but one of which (The Mustard Seed, also in Mark 4:30–32, Luke 13:18–19) are unique to Matthew. How are the four parables without explanations clarified by those with explanations?

18b: What, in your reading, remains obscure or open to a variety of interpretations in these messages about the kingdom of heaven?

Read Luke 10:29–37

18c: A little historical background helps to set the stage for the Parable of the Good Samaritan. Priests and Levites were religious officials chosen from certain families to administer the system of temple sacrifice. You will recall from our survey of intertestamental history (chapter 12) that Samaritans were considered abhorrent by conservative Jews. How is this parable both an ethical lesson and an indictment of the religious establishment?

Read Luke 14:7–24

18d: The Parables of the Wedding Feast (14:7–14) and the Great Banquet (14:15–24; parallel Matt 22:1–14), like the Parable of the Good Samaritan, can be construed either as moral lessons or as judgment of the religious establishment. What is the strongest argument you can make from the content and context of these parables for both interpretations?

Read Luke 15:11–32

18e: The Parable of the Prodigal Son is perhaps the most famous of Jesus' parables, but some would argue that it should be called the Parable of Two Sons, because of the importance of the elder son. Again, the primary message is ambiguous: is it about God's mercy, the need for repentance, or an indictment of the religious establishment? How do the content and composition of the parable weigh in favor of one of these approaches?

Read Luke 16:19–31

18f: The Parable of the Rich Man and Lazarus is the only parable that names a character, perhaps because it is so easy to group and dismiss the "nameless" poor. Given the presence in Luke of so much teaching about the dangers of wealth, including vv. 10–15 just before the parable, there are obvious ethical implications here. Are there indications in the parable and in Luke's other parables, however, that the "rich man" may be interpreted more broadly?

Read Luke 18:10–14

18g: It is fitting to end our consideration with the Parable of the Pharisee and the Tax Collector, because the story pulls together, in less than a hundred words, the two major parable themes of religious and moral contrast. Pharisees were admired for their knowledge of Scripture and passionate devotion to righteousness. Tax collectors were especially despised because they were natives, empowered to add self-enriching surcharges on top of the amount they had bid to satisfy Roman authorities. One detail lost in translation is that the tax collector refers to himself literally as *the* sinner, not *a* sinner. What are at least three other details for each of the two characters that highlight the contrast between them?

Approaching the Bible as Literature

For Further Study:

1. Note that Matthew and Luke follow Mark in placing the Parable of the Sower early in Jesus' ministry. But in Matthew's case, it follows rather than precedes Jesus' first major discourse, the Sermon on the Mount. From a literary point of view, what is the logic of this sequence: discipleship first, kingdom second?

2. What differences do you note between the two main clusters of kingdom parables in Matthew, and what differences help to explain the placement of the second group near the end of the Gospel?

3. Compare the use of these narrative techniques in the longer parables: monologue, dialogue, two- or three-part sequences of action, and setting details.

4. After considering most or all of the parables, explain what would be gained or lost if we had no teachings of Jesus other than parables. How full would be our picture of Jesus' beliefs about the kingdom and about discipleship?

5. Based on your study of the parables in this chapter, compose a parable of the kingdom and a parable of discipleship using both the features outlined in the previous chapter and the themes considered in this chapter.

6. How, in your opinion, does modern popular or religious use of the more famous parables (Sower, Good Samaritan, Prodigal Son, Lazarus) reflect or distort the original intent of these stories?

Section Seven

Epistle as Window into the
Life of the Early Church

Chapter 19

The Epistle and Community Construction

Technically, there are no epistles in the New Testament. As a literary term, *epistle* refers to an essay or verse composition that takes the form of a letter to treat moral or philosophical issues. In the Roman world, Seneca, Horace, and Cicero were known for their epistles. In biblical studies, the term *epistle* is applied to a body of New Testament writings that are in fact genuine letters, addressing real people and situations.

Letter writing was a common activity for people in the Roman world. We have thousands of surviving examples, the vast majority only a few sentences in length. Just as correspondence today follows certain conventions, so in the ancient world—and in fact, the pattern is quite similar. An ancient letter begins with a salutation, an expression of thanksgiving for or good wishes to the recipient, the main message (expressed in conventional language), and a farewell formula. There was rarely a signature.

The New Testament includes thirteen New Testament letters attributed to Paul, an anonymous letter "to the Hebrews," one to James, two to Peter, three to John, and one to Jude.

Together, these works make up about 40 percent of the New Testament, and they provide a treasure of information about the circumstances, beliefs, and practices of the early Christians. But why study them from a literary perspective *as letters*?

Innovation in New Testament Epistles

We begin by noting the departure of New Testament epistles from the familiar pattern of first-century letter writing. Except for Paul's letter to Philemon, 2–3 John, and Jude, the New Testament letters are significantly longer, up to fifteen pages in modern translation. Paul and others expand the conventional main message feature of the personal letter into lengthy treatment of behavioral issues, doctrinal distinctions, and appeals for unity.

Paul's expanded treatment of ethical and doctrinal disputes looks similar in many ways to the epistles of Seneca, Horace, and Cicero. But his extended personal treatment of real issues in the community, his lack of interest in literary vocabulary and style, and his sometimes-lengthy personal greetings are all far removed from the formal, stylized approach of his Roman contemporaries.

Although Paul's style may be personal and non-literary, it is clear that he writes as an apostle, an authority figure who assumes that his letters will be read aloud to the community and will carry great weight. This assumption is common to all of the New Testament epistles. Even the author of the more essay-like Hebrews, who is anonymous, writes as one who expects his audience to comply with his instruction. The letters also present long arguments and rhetorical devices to enhance their persuasive effect. In all of these respects, the New Testament epistles possess a quasi-official character not present in other non-literary letters of the Roman world.

Combining the innovative features, what emerges is a new genre. It may be that the New Testament epistle as we know it was invented or adapted by Paul to unite and build communities whose leaders tended to "train on the job" while their founders and other experts traveled on to begin other communities. Letters from apostles and their associates that were both personal and authoritative would borrow from different existing letter forms to serve the community needs. Paul's approach may have originated from Jewish letters similarly designed to provide instruction and promote unity among the far-flung members of the Jewish *diaspora*. While possible examples are few and the research recent, scholars may eventually show that Paul's Jewish background is an important aspect of the development of the New Testament epistles.

Closer Inspection

An aspect of literary analysis that has yielded much information about early Christianity is the close scrutiny of ways in which New Testament writers customize the traditional letter-writing elements in their epistles. For example, Paul changes the standard opening, "greetings" (*chairein*), to "grace and peace" (*charis kai eirene*); this is not only a pun in the first term but also a double dose of Paul's new Christian doctrine of grace and his Jewish heritage of *shalom* (Hebrew for "peace"). He often adds to his greeting in ways that introduce the content of the letter. For example, in his letter to the Galatians, he anticipates his opponents' argument that he is a second-tier authority and opens "Paul an apostle—sent neither by human commission nor from human authorities . . . and all those who are with me." Only after thus staking his claim does Paul continue with "grace and peace."

Paul also expands the standard expression of thanksgiving and well-wishes, the ancient equivalent of "having a good time, wish you were here." In 1 Thessalonians, Paul launches into a half-page expression of detailed gratitude for the community; in 2 Corinthians, he writes an entire page on the theme of comfort related to his own and the community's sufferings.

Paul's letters often end with long lists of greetings, as boring to the casual reader as biblical genealogies, but revealing to scholars much insight into early Christianity. The chapter-length list of personal greetings at the end of Romans is remarkable given the fact that Paul had never visited Rome: clearly, he and many of his addressees had traveled extensively in order to build up such an extensive network of relationships. These and other personal greetings in the epistles also yield data to scholars of ancient names, which are often linked to ethnic and socio-economic status. Experts can associate names in New Testament letters with demographic distinctions, just as you might make reasonable deductions about the diversity of a group that includes Billy Bob Duke, Deshawna Williams, Abe Cohen, and Hunter "Biff" Brookings III.

Questions about authorship of some New Testament epistles sometimes center on differences in style, vocabulary, and content either between the letters of one author (Paul or Peter) or on the likelihood that a writer with presumably humble origins could produce a sophisticated letter (James, Peter, and John). Authorship in the ancient world was a complex matter. Paul, for example, is quite open about his employment of an *amanuensis*, or writing secretary, for the composition of his letters. This was in fact an ancient and accepted practice: a man named Baruch wrote the book of Jeremiah (Jer 36:4). In Rom 16:2, Tertius names himself as the writer; similarly, 1 Peter states that "I have written . . . through Sylvanus" (5:12). Where Paul does not mention an amanuensis, his brief "I write this in my own hand" (1 Cor 16:21; Gal 6:11; Col 4:18; 2 Thess 3:19; Philemon 19) implies an amanuensis and serves as the equivalent of the modern political ad ending: "I am [the candidate,] and I endorse this message." How much editorial freedom did the amanuensis have? Furthermore, who else was involved forming the content of the epistles—named or unnamed? In most of Paul's letters, he adds to the opening greeting the name or names of co-senders, and it is not clear what role these others might have played in the composition of the letters.

Reasoning Backward from Form to Situation

A branch of literary analysis known as *form criticism* attempts to reconstruct the original situation that produced a piece of writing by studying its final *form*. Imagine, for example, that you happen upon a crumbled piece paper in a school hallway that reads as follows: "Dear Fred, Lately I've been under a lot of stress, and I need some space to discover who I am. Don't get me wrong, I respect you and will always enjoy the great times we've had, but can't we be just friends for a while and see others without being threatened? All the best, Marsha." This is what scholars of doomed romance call a "Dear John" letter, and we all recognize the cliché-ridden phrases of the form that reveal the tragic reality of the situation: Marsha has found another guy.

Form criticism of the New Testament is most commonly applied to the Gospels in an attempt to understand what situation in the life of the early Christians caused them to preserve, arrange, or (according to some critics) invent aspects of the life and teachings of Jesus. When the method is applied to Acts and the epistles, it may yield less speculative results, because we can cross reference epistles with other epistles, Acts, and sometimes non-biblical sources of information. The form of the set speech sermon, for example, might generate all kinds of speculation if we had only an isolated example. But the multiple sermons in Acts, supplemented by similar material in 1Cor 15, clarified still further by doctrinal passages in Romans and Galatians, allow us to understand more fully the need to articulate the essential message in the final form that the text presents: as a series of events that is well attested and fulfills God's plan. Similarly, the so-called "household tables" (Eph 5–6, Col 3, 1 Tim 2, 1 Pet 2–3), which give instructions for relations between people at different levels of family and society, may have arisen to reassure new converts or outsiders that Christianity had an ordered ethical approach and would not undermine society. Consideration of these tables together, and viewing them in light of general instructions about release from legalism (Rom 5–8, Gal 2–5), helps the reader to appreciate the tension between accountability and freedom in the lives of the first Christians.

Approaching the Bible as Literature

For Further Study:

1. Using the elements described above for Roman era letters, compose a brief epistle for a friend or group on an issue or event of importance to you.

2. Research the epistles of Seneca, Horace, or Cicero. How do they compare to Paul's letters in terms of style and content? Based on your study, could Paul have modeled his correspondence after these works?

3. Consider the elements of epistolary writing in 2 Macc 1:1—2:18; how does this passage compare to Paul's style and content?

4. What are the advantages and disadvantages of conducting a relationship today by letter or email? How do these factors differ if the relationship is with a group or an individual? How would these problems differ in the ancient world as compared to the modern world?

5. Research onomatology (the study of names) in relation to the people Paul greets in Rom 16; what do you learn about his addressees?

6. Apply the principles of form criticism to a film like *The Wizard of Oz*, *Spartacus*, or *Jesus Christ Superstar*. Explain in detail what situation in American life gave rise to the form of this film.

7. Research the early second-century epistles of either the Roman Pliny the Elder or the Christian Ignatius of Antioch and compare them to Paul's epistles in terms of the style features described here.

Chapter 20

A Brief History of Early Christianity

The Opening Act of Acts

In order to set the stage for a consideration of the contents of the New Testament epistles, it is useful to survey the beginnings of the Christian movement. Much of our information is taken from the book of Acts, the purpose of which is to describe the advance of the gospel message from Jerusalem to Rome. It is evident that the author chooses this narrow focus after chapter 8 when, instead of continuing with events in Jerusalem and elsewhere, he begins to concentrate on the career of Paul and to move the narrative toward its geographic goal. This choice may be due to Rome's importance in the first-century world, so that once the gospel arrives there it is officially "universal." The dominant interest in the legitimacy of Christianity in Roman legal terms may be another reason for this focus.

There is no reason to dispute the early church tradition that the same Luke who wrote the Gospel wrote Acts. He begins with a dedication to Theophilus and a reference to a former book; vocabulary and content also link the two. Some scholars speculate that Luke may have been involved in Paul's legal proceedings, because events and speeches in later chapters reflect detailed knowledge or even documents from the litigation. Acts ends abruptly with Paul still awaiting a final trial in Rome, which may indicate either that Luke had written up to the events that had occurred, or that Paul had already been killed but Luke did not consider the apostle's death a suitable ending for the work.

Acts is entirely narrative with the exception of a number of sermons by key characters which reveal the essential content of their preaching, or *kerygma*. (Even in the New Testament itself, the essential message is commonly called the *gospel* with a lower case *g*, as distinguished from one of the four Gospels.) The key elements of the kerygma are that Jesus fulfilled the Old Testament, performed miracles, was crucified and resurrected according to God's plan, will return as humanity's judge, and requires that individuals repent, believe, and receive baptism as a sign of membership in the community of believers. The self-designation of the initial group, incidentally, was the *Way* (9:2; 18:25; 19:9; 19:23; 22:4; 24:14; 24:22), presumably referring to the way or manner of salvation and discipleship.

The sequence of events in Acts, while not a complete history of the early decades of the Christian movement, gives us considerable information. The narrative begins with Jesus ascending into heaven several weeks after his resurrection. Soon after this, the apostles, who had gathered together with a number of other believers, "received the Spirit" and became bold preachers who began to organize for mutual aid and instruction and to mobilize to expand the movement. Technically, this reception of God's Spirit, named Pentecost for the Jewish holiday with which its occurrence coincided, is the beginning of Christianity. The movement was immediately controversial. Although the first believers were all Jews, religious authorities in Jerusalem were as resistant to the group as they were to Jesus, and some of the early believers and their leaders were persecuted or killed. One zealous young Pharisee named Saul, on his way to Damascus to round up some of these religious rebels, instead encountered the risen Jesus on the road and converted to the new faith. He soon took on the Greek name Paul and began to preach far and wide in support of the faith he once opposed.

The Way Moves Away

Before returning to Paul, it is important to understand how and where Christianity was spread by others. The record in Acts suggests that the first missionaries went north to Samaria (8:1–39), then Damascus (9:2), Galilee (9:31), Joppa (9:36–43), Caesarea (10:1—11:18), Phoenecia, Cyprus, and Antioch (11:19–26). In most cases, the movement involved conversion of Jews to the belief that Jesus was the messiah. But the religious establishment, and increasingly the militant element among the Jews, continued to oppose Christianity. When Jews in Palestine rebelled against Rome in the mid-60s AD, the Christian community in Jerusalem under the leadership of Jesus' cousin Simeon moved north to escape the conflict. By the time of the second major Jewish rebellion in AD 132–136, the Christian presence in Palestine was minimal. Instead, through the first century and beyond, missionaries traveled extensively to Jewish communities in the north and east (modern Turkey, Syria, and Iraq) to establish numerous Christian communities on the eastern fringes of the Roman Empire and beyond. Other areas where Christianity took hold early were parts of the Roman Empire with established Jewish populations: Greece, Asia Minor, northern Egypt, the northwest coast of Africa, and southern Spain. We should not view the establishment of Christianity as a smooth, inexorable, or altogether unified movement. Surviving documents, including the New Testament, indicate that there were controversies and splinter groups from the beginning. Some demanded closer allegiance to the Jewish law or radical demands of Jesus, and others were heavily influenced by Greco-Roman religion and philosophy. By the second century, Gnosticism, based largely on Plato's dualistic view of the spirit as higher than or superior to the physical realm, was a major alternative form of Christianity. These and other interesting developments, however, lie beyond the scope of our inquiry.

The book of Acts, from chapter 13 on, covers almost exclusively the activities of Paul. While little is known of his early preaching, the narrative of Acts covers in detail Paul's three major missionary journeys (AD 45–58) through the eastern Mediterranean region, mostly in the larger cities of modern Turkey and Greece. These were important population and commercial centers, each with a Jewish community where Paul would always begin his preaching; however, he found more receptive audiences among the gentiles. It is important to note that early Christianity was a fundamentally urban movement that spread from cities to the countryside. It is also worthy of note that, from the beginning, converts came from a cross section of society—not only the slave and free working classes, but also some rich and influential people who provided financial aid, houses in which to meet, and political protection. Acts and Paul's letters name a number of these individuals from the higher social strata. Finally, it is evident from the mid-first century onward that Christians gradually shifted the focus of missionary efforts from Jewish to gentile populations. In fact, some of the churches established by Paul may have been gentile in the majority almost from the beginning.

Acts after Acts

Following Paul's missionary journeys, he was imprisoned in Caesarea (the Roman base in Palestine) for two years for supposed sedition. After appealing his case to Caesar, he traveled under guard to Rome for his eventual trial and death, which took place AD 64–67. What we know of Paul (and other apostles) beyond the New Testament record comes in part from relatively reliable contemporary Christian writings and in part from sources written long after with pious embellishments, making it difficult to distinguish fact from invention. Paul was probably released from Roman imprisonment for a brief period, and reliable sources report that he preached in the Roman provinces of Spain before returning to Rome, where he was beheaded by order of emperor Nero (Whether Paul actually spoke with Nero is unknown). There is good evidence that the apostle Peter was killed in Rome about the same time, in the area where the Vatican now stands. This period also marks the first undisputed reference to Christianity on the part of a non-Christian writer: the Roman historian Tacitus, writing in the early second century AD, accuses Nero of making Christians the scapegoats for a major fire in central Rome (AD 64) and conducting a violent persecution for several months; the timing makes this a likely explanation for the deaths of Paul and Peter.

Information about the later lives of other apostles is sketchy, but there is enough reliable information to suggest that a number of them traveled throughout the Roman world and well beyond its borders to the east, perhaps as far as India. Meanwhile, the original Christian group in Jerusalem was in conflict with Jewish religious authorities and the forces of rebellion against Rome. Before armed conflict destroyed the city and temple in AD 70, Jerusalem Christians moved north as a group; and by the end of the first century, the Christian movement was fading in Palestine just as it was spreading rapidly elsewhere, from Spain to Persia and from Britain to Egypt.

For Further Study:

1. Why does the conversion of the first gentiles in Caesarea (Acts 10–11) occupy so much space in the narrative, and what issues does this narrative both review and foreshadow?

2. Compare the account of Paul in Acts 13–28 with the picture of him gained from one of his more personal letters (e.g., Galatians, 2 Corinthians) and discuss Luke's portrait of his style and personality.

3. Research the abrupt ending of Acts in terms of style and content. What is the majority view and its weaknesses?

4. Research the death of either Paul or Peter. What features of the literature contribute to challenges of historicity, and how are these different or similar to New Testament documents?

Chapter 21

Style and Content in the Epistles

In this chapter, we will consider four representative epistles: two by Paul, one by James, and one by John. The purpose of this selection is to show the variety of style and content in the New Testament letters. Following our study of these four, I will summarize the other epistles in canonical order.

Of the twenty-one letters in the New Testament, Paul's thirteen are presented first, in order of length to groups and then to individuals. Hebrews follows, then James, two letters by Peter, three by John, and Jude. This may seem an arbitrary organizational scheme, but it is hard to imagine a better one. There is much debate concerning the chronological order in which the letters were composed, and that is partly due to dispute of traditional authorship for half the letters. There is broad consensus, however, that Galatians is an authentic letter of Paul composed about AD 50, and that Romans was written by Paul from Corinth near the end of his third missionary journey, about AD 56.

Re-convincing the Galatians

The church in Galatia, which included believers in several cities in what is now south-central Turkey, was established by Paul in the late 40s during his first missionary journey. But alternate forms of Christian belief, probably promoted by other traveling Christian preachers, began to sway the group from Paul's teaching. These opponents, which scholars refer to as *Judaizers*, insisted that gentile converts receive circumcision and practice strict observance of the Old Testament law. Paul probably learned of this development by report in Jerusalem, where a critical conference of Christian leaders was about to take place that would affirm Paul's teaching and leadership (Acts 15). This is the historical context for this short work's major theme, that salvation comes by faith and not by works of the law (good deeds).

Paul's structure in Galatians is straightforward: an autobiographical argument for salvation by faith (chapters 1–2), a theological argument for salvation by faith (chapter 3–4), and a discussion of the ethical implications of salvation by faith (5–6); the epistle closes with a lengthy personal greeting confirming Paul's endorsement of the letter (6:11–18).

Style and Content in the Epistles

Read Galatians 1–6

21a: What expressions and writing techniques does Paul use to express emotion (cite specifics), and what is the result in terms of the tone of the letter?

21b: Paul employs several kinds of argument in chapter 3–4 to make his theological point. What would be the strengths and weaknesses of this approach for his original audience?

21c: Gal 3:28 has been called one of the key statements in the entire New Testament. In what sense would it be considered revolutionary then, and what are its implications for later historical developments?

STYLE AND CONTENT IN THE EPISTLES

Self-introduction to the Romans

The purpose of Paul's letter to the Romans is to introduce the apostle by explaining the gospel that he preaches. By the mid-fifties AD, Christianity had been established in Rome by other missionaries, and believers may have numbered in the thousands, but Paul had not yet visited the great city. His extended exposition of the substance of the faith is intended to confirm his standing as an apostle who may be helpful to the Roman Christians, and possibly to anticipate his request for financial aid to continue his travels. Paul does not address problems in the Roman church, but his lengthy list of personal greetings (ch 16) indicates considerable knowledge about the group. The implications of this letter and other sources are that the Roman Christians were ethnically mixed, perhaps about half converts from the large Jewish population in the city (estimated at up to fifty thousand), half gentiles from a mix of slaves and the free working classes, and a few wealthy and well-connected individuals. In fact, hints from Roman sources suggest that there were a few Christian converts at the highest levels of society who provided financial and political aid for the community.

Romans begins with an extended theological section that is sometimes called "the gospel according to Paul" (ch 1–8). The next few chapters address the issue of Jews in relation to Christianity (ch 9–11); Paul believes they are still "chosen" and will come around eventually. The epistle ends with a description of the implications of belief for conduct (ch 12–15) and a long list of personal greetings (ch 16).

Before reading the early chapters of Romans, it is helpful to gain some familiarity with some key terms. Because Paul's theological vocabulary is subtle and complex, and his meanings have occupied scholars for two thousand years, the beginner should regard this as an introductory explanation. Paul assigns distinct functions to God the Father, God the Son, and God the Spirit—what Christian writers later called the Trinity, which understands God existing as one nature in three persons. We might understand this in terms of an electrical appliance, where the Father is the power source, the Son is the appliance that we see, and the Spirit is the electricity that makes the appliance work on peoples' behalf. In Paul's understanding, God chose the death of Jesus to accomplish salvation for all those who receive it as a gift; it cannot be earned by good behavior or "works." In Paul's terms, God *elects, predestines*, or *foreknows* those who will receive the gift of salvation, which is also called *justification, redemption*, or *reconciliation*. An individual who receives salvation is forgiven for past and future sin (wrongdoing) and is considered righteous in God's eyes. Paul maintains that this does not involve a license to further sin; rather, salvation results in a transformed life in which the Spirit accomplishes *sanctification* ("making holy"); and after death, *glorification*, the final reward of perfection and communion with God. This explanation raises obvious questions about the interplay of God's will and human will, both in initial belief and in the subsequent process of spiritual growth. These are among the ongoing questions for Paul's interpreters.

Paul begins his explanation with a two-part statement of the problem faced by humanity of alienation from God. In 1:18—2:16, he argues on the basis of natural law that gentiles are alienated from God even though they do not understand why; in 2:17—3:20, he offers an extended argument that Jews are guilty too, even though they are largely obedient to the law that God has revealed. Having established the problem, Paul moves into the solution in successive sections about justification (3:21—5:21), sanctification (6:1—8:17), and glorification (8:18–39).

Read Romans 1–8

21d: How does the prologue (1:1–17) function in terms of Paul's purposes for the letter as described above?

21e: Paul's description of struggle with sin (7:7–25) appears to convey a more personal tone than the surrounding doctrinal material. In your opinion, is Paul employing a technique to strengthen his argument; and if the section is autobiographical, does it appear more likely in the context to describe Paul's past or current struggle? Explain your response.

21f: How does the tone change in chapter 8, what techniques are employed to express it, and how does the shift in tone affect the persuasiveness of Paul's argument?

Read Romans 12–14

21g: This section is typical of Paul's moral instruction, which usually follows treatments of doctrine or controversy in the community. Among the noteworthy passages here is the juxtaposition of 12:14–21, which has traditionally been cited to justify pacifism; and 13:1–7, which has traditionally been cited to justify Christian participation in war. Can you reconcile Paul's statements into a unified approach to the issue?

Style and Content in the Epistles

James: Salvation by Works?

It is instructive to consider the epistle of James following Romans, because this pairing highlights the diversity of perspective in early Christianity. The Reformer Martin Luther found the focus on behavior in James so troubling that he called it an "epistle of straw" and resisted including it in the Bible. But the early church accepted the tension, which is analogous in some ways to the juxtaposition in the Old Testament of books like Deuteronomy and Job or Ecclesiastes. Is there unity in such diversity? This is a challenging question for interpreters.

James (a Latinized English translation of the Hebrew and Greek name "Jacob") was a common name in New Testament times. James the apostle was killed in AD 42, too early to have written this epistle. After the apostle's martyrdom, James the brother of Jesus became the leader of the Jerusalem church until he was killed in AD 62. This does not guarantee that the James mentioned in the first verse of the epistle is the same person, especially since the book was used and accepted relatively late compared to other epistles. Perhaps the best argument for early composition by the James who led the Jerusalem church is that the epistle contains numerous commands similar to teachings of Jesus in the Gospels but does not *quote* them—suggesting that the Gospels were not yet written. In any case, the letter is clear in its purpose, which is to offer general instructions about living. Of 108 verses, sixty involve direct commands in the imperative mood. Clearly, the author intends to show that right conduct is the only legitimate way to express one's faith.

Read James 1–5

21h: What statements about works in relation to faith in James 1–2 appear to contradict Paul's statements in Galatians 2 and Romans 5–8, and is it possible to reconcile these statements?

Approaching the Bible as Literature

1 John and the Command to Love

The first epistle of John contends that true belief involves love for other believers in response to the love of Jesus. The letter is anonymous, but early church tradition attributed the letter to the apostle John. The similarities of vocabulary and style between 1 John and the Gospel confirm authorship by the same person, so authorship questions about both works are often considered together. In terms of content, this general letter responds to an early form of *Gnostic* thought that eventually came to rival orthodox belief. These "antichrists" (2:18, 22; 4:3), believing that matter is evil, denied the physical reality of Jesus, who in their view only *seemed* human. This *docetism* (from the Greek verb "to seem"), according to critics like John, resulted in disregard for the activities of the body, including immorality and lack of love. This background sets the epistle accurately in the context of controversy with implications for behavior, not merely an appeal for mutual affection.

Unlike other New Testament epistles, 1 John moves around its subject in a free-associative style more typical of Jewish rabbinic writing than a methodical and linear structure influenced by Greek literature.

Read 1 John 1–5

21i: The most obvious literary technique in this epistle is repetition. What terms and phrases are commonly used to address the readers and to formulate commands, and how do these affect the tone of the letter?

21j: What statements does the writer make that directly contradict the principles of Gnosticism as outlined above?

Other New Testament Epistles

1 Corinthians is a lengthy exhortation by Paul that focuses on unity and responsible behavior. Corinth was a large, prosperous port with a reputation for decadence, factors which may explain the issues faced by the church. The first four chapters address church factions; then Paul offers extended instruction regarding sexual misconduct (chapters 5–7), insensitive behavior (8–11), disorder in worship (12–14), and denial of the resurrection (15), followed by a chapter of personal greetings. The ongoing relevance of these issues makes 1 Corinthians one of the most influential New Testament works, and its famous "love chapter" (13) is often quoted at weddings—although the original direction was toward a congregation, not a married couple.

2 Corinthians addresses the church's rebellion against Paul and their subsequent reconciliation; the last few highly emotional chapters may have been joined later from a separate letter. Between these lengthy treatments of personal issues between the church and the apostle is a passionate appeal to support Paul's financial collection for the poor in Jerusalem (ch 8–9).

Ephesians, Philippians, Colossians, and *Philemon* are called the Prison Epistles because of Paul's circumstances when he wrote them. They treat general theological and behavioral concerns of churches under Paul's care. *Philemon*, the only one-page letter by Paul that survives, encourages a Christian slave owner to release his runaway slave, who has encountered Paul after becoming a believer. It took far too long, but this letter had an important influence on the abolition of slavery.

1 Thessalonians congratulates believers for their faithfulness and provides instruction on several matters, most importantly the *Parousia* or second coming of Christ, which was evidently a cause of some confusion for this new group of converts. *2 Thessalonians* was probably written very soon after as a follow up, offering further clarification and warning against dissent.

The Pastoral Epistles, *1–2 Timothy* and *Titus*, are so named because they are addressed to ministers under Paul's supervision. They are intended to arm church leaders in their struggle against false teaching.

Hebrews is an anonymous essay, not quite a letter, but it includes several important features of the epistle, including repeated reference to issues facing a particular group and a closing with personal information and greetings. The work is widely regarded as the most literary book in the New Testament, characterized by a high level of Greek, sophisticated argumentation, and much word play. Its purpose is to urge this potentially backsliding group of believers to persevere in the face of opposition by growth in knowledge and right behavior.

James, 1–2 Peter, 1–3 John, and *Jude* are called the General or Catholic Epistles because they are written to Christians "generally"; that is, to believers distributed over a wide geographic area. You will note that, unlike other New Testament letters, they take their names from their writers and not from their recipients. *1–2 Peter* are intended to arm believers against hostility from outsiders or heretical teaching by encouraging hope and right conduct. *Jude*, very similar in content to 2 Peter, warns against false teachers who promote immorality. *2–3 John* are one-page letters clearly written by the author of 1 John and the Gospel, who here calls himself "the elder," and they are directed toward specific churches to adjudicate in some dispute. Their brevity and lack of new material caused early debate about including them in the Bible; but ultimately, the conviction that they were penned by an apostle led to their inclusion.

For Further Study:

1. Consider Paul's theological argument for the afterlife in 1 Corinthians 15. What are the techniques and bases of his position, and what are its strengths and weaknesses for a modern audience?

2. Paul uses the word "law" in at least five senses in Romans alone. Explore these nuances, and consider Paul's use of the words *law* and *works* in light of his own background as a Pharisee.

3. Research the composition of 2 Corinthians in light of the dramatic shift in tone after chapter 9. Is the current form of the epistle original, or were separate letters joined; and if so, by whom and when?

4. Research Greek rhetorical style and rabbinic argument and find examples of both in Paul's letters or in Hebrews.

5. Scholars agree that key themes in Paul include describing the nature of Christ, explaining justification, guiding Christian conduct, Paul's relation to Judaism, and expectations regarding the future. Choosing any two letters, illustrate these themes and discuss how they might be prioritized.

6. Find instruction on a specific topic of behavior in the epistles (e.g., forgiveness, dangers of wealth, nonviolence, response to persecution) and compare to Jesus' teaching; what similarities and difference are there?

7. Research the social makeup of the churches addressed in 1 Corinthians or Romans; how does that information affect the understanding of the issues addressed?

8. Research the tone of Paul's letters when he addressed both opponents and supporters; how does this study help to construct a personal portrait of Paul?

9. Discuss the similarities between Gnosticism and Eastern or New Age thought; do the problems and criticisms of the New Testament writers apply to these different versions of reality?

Section Eight

Apocalyptic and Future Hope
in the Book of Revelation

Chapter 22

Apocalyptic and Prophecy in the New Testament

Early Christian Expectations

Apocalyptic writing and expectations regarding the end of history were central for the first Christians. For several centuries, they scrutinized the Old Testament book of Daniel and intertestamental pseudepigrapha, mulled over the relevant New Testament passages, and composed new apocalyptic works. By contrast, Jews stopped writing and reading apocalyptic literature after their terrible experience of trying to hasten the end by engaging in armed rebellion against Rome, partly under the influence of these writings. Christians were consistently opposed to violence for the first few centuries of the movement, but they hoped that God would act on their behalf and set up the kingdom promised by Jesus. They understood the life of Christ in first-century Palestine as his *first* coming, which accomplished salvation for those who would trust in him; but salvation would ultimately be delivered at Christ's *second* coming, when he would usher in a new age. This approach allowed Christians then and now to view biblical predictive prophecy in two or even three stages: some events would occur in biblical times, while others would occur either spread out over history or near the end as signs of its imminence. Needless to say, deciding which event is which, and how to interpret highly symbolic language in terms of historical events, has kept interpreters busy ever since. Under the influence of biblical material about the end of time, many believers have lived in a perpetual sense of readiness, but some have experienced embarrassment over misguided predictions regarding historical figures and exact dates.

The "Little Apocalypse" of Jesus

The Synoptic Gospels record a number of statements by Jesus consistent with apocalyptic expectations and one lengthy eschatological discourse which is sometimes called the "little apocalypse." This passage is a triple tradition, occurring in substantially the same form in Matt 24:1–51; Mark 13:1–37; and Luke 21:5–36. Read any of these and note several familiar features of the apocalyptic genre: cosmic struggle,

God's intervention, messianic focus, and reward of the elect. Observe also the statements that give rise to questions of immediate versus later fulfillment.

What is distinctive in the Gospel passages as compared to Daniel, Revelation, and many pseudepigraphal works is the realism of Jesus' predictions. While the Gospel apocalypses predict the end of time and reward for the elect, there is little symbolism and little that might be construed as a vision. Some interpreters insist that the Synoptics must have been written after the destruction of the temple (AD 70) in order to account for Jesus' predictions in this and the parallel passages in the other two synoptic Gospels. The fact is, these predictions might be made by any contemporary Palestinian with an accurate sense of the political climate and the likely results of rebellion against Roman power. Further, Jesus' language echoes that of Old Testament prophets in their descriptions of previous destructions of Jerusalem. As a literary feature consistent with other apocalyptic writing, this may account for the predictions better than after-the-fact composition.

Apocalyptic does not usually demand a response on the part of the audience, because it assumes that the lines have already been drawn, that the audience is merely waiting for God to administer punishment and reward (e.g., 1 Enoch, ch 14 above). But Jesus' message, and that of Revelation, conveys a strong admonition to practice one's faith during the waiting period. As we will see, "Keep awake" in Jesus' terms is expanded into detailed instructions for believers in Revelation 1–2.

Prophecy in the New Testament

The eschatological discourse and related sayings of Jesus (e.g., Matt 11:20–24; 13:36–43; Luke 12:41–56; 17:20–37) are joined by several future predictive prophetic passages in the epistles; the most important of these are 1 Cor 15:51–58; 2 Cor 5:1–10; 1 Thess 4:13–5:11; 2 Thess 2:1–12; and 2 Pet 3:8–13. But everywhere in the New Testament there is a tone of expectation regarding future eschatological hope, even where the coming of Christ is not mentioned. As strange as it may seem to us, this tone was part of the mindset of the New Testament audience. Because sudden hardship and disease were common, and persecution or war could loom suddenly, death was an ever-present reality, not a distant misfortune largely reserved for the elderly. Furthermore, expectations that God would soon intervene in history were fueled by dramatic world events that religious leaders understood in terms of the end of time. These factors lent a sense of urgency to religious belief and conduct.

It is also important to point out that in the New Testament as in the Old Testament, a prophet does not function exclusively or even primarily as a predictor of the future but as an interpreter of the present. This is clearly the case in Paul's extended discussion of the function of prophecy in the Corinthian church (1Cor 14) and in brief references elsewhere (e.g., Mark 14:65; Acts 21:9; Eph 4:11; 1 Thess 5:20; 1 Tim 4:14; 1John 4:1). It is evident from these and some early non-canonical Christian writings that prophets functioned primarily to deliver messages to the believing community directly from God. For obvious reasons, such figures—especially those who moved from place to place—were carefully examined to determine the consistency of their message with Scripture and with their own conduct.

For Further Study:

1. How are the apocalyptic passages in the Gospels like or unlike the material in Daniel, 1 Enoch, and Revelation?

2. What specific statements in Jesus' "little apocalypse" are ambiguous in terms of immediate or long term fulfillment, and for what audience: the original hearers, later first-century Christians, or readers much later?

3. Research the passages in Paul's and Peter's letters and classify them as apocalyptic or future prophetic. How do they differ from, clarify, or complicate Jesus' teaching about the eschaton?

4. Some have interpreted the New Testament message about the eschaton "spiritually" or figuratively as a reference to the vibrant new life of the believer rather than to a future time. How would you evaluate this view in light of the original intent and original recipients of these writings?

5. Research the "problem of delay" of Christ's second coming in early Christianity, and evaluate the major solutions.

6. Research the role of prophet in the New Testament era and historically since. What is the function, how is a prophet distinguished from a preacher or missionary, and what dangers led to close evaluation of prophets?

Chapter 23

Image and Message in Revelation

Apocalyptic Features and Departures

How convenient to end our consideration of the Bible with the book of Revelation, which not only exemplifies the apocalyptic genre and describes the culmination of history but also brings us full circle to review important features of Old Testament writing. Indeed, one of the first features about Revelation to observe is that it constantly employs terminology, style, and images from the Old Testament prophets but never actually quotes them. This is part of the book's evocation of authority, mystery, and meaning.

This Old Testament *flavor* is also part of what signals Revelation as an example of the apocalyptic genre. Like works such as Daniel and 1 Enoch, Revelation delivers its message in rough Greek that approximates the "antiquated" style of prophets who wrote centuries earlier. And like these works, Revelation features a series of visions that employ heavily symbolic language to reveal the coming cosmic struggle in which God will triumph and reward the elect.

But Revelation differs from other apocalyptic works in at least two important respects. First, it names its author not as an important figure from the past but as John, a contemporary: either the apostle or some other recognized leader with that name. This constitutes a claim of validity for the book from the start. That is, the audience is not encountering a work of pious fiction but the report of actual visions given in a particular place, the nearby island of Patmos, by someone living in their time whom they presumably knew (1:9–11).

Closely linked to the feature of contemporary authorship is the significance of the book's structure. The primary message of Revelation is contained in the letters to seven churches in chapters 2–3. These are real churches, listed in a geographical circle beginning with the large city of Ephesus, the closest port to the island of Patmos, where the visions are reported to have occurred. The circular list may represent the route of the book's delivery and explanation by its writer or carrier. More importantly, the content of the letters is not the self-congratulatory "we are the good guys" message typical of apocalyptic writing, but a sometimes-biting exhortation for the audience to persevere in the face of difficulties. Indeed, the logical structure of the work is summarized in 1:3: "Blessed are those who hear and who keep what is written [in chapters 2–3]; for the time is near [for the events described in chapters 4–22]. This may be a surprise to those who assume that Revelation is all about the future; instead, the book regards the future as the reason to act responsibly in the present.

While there is some dispute about whether the John of Revelation is the same John associated with the Gospel and epistles, there is general agreement that the book was composed toward the end of Emperor Domitian's reign, AD 90–95. Although names are all in code (Rome, for example, is "the whore of Babylon" in chapter 17–18), the situation in the text reflects this period, which saw the first empire-wide persecution of Christians. In fact, this region was a center of emperor worship, which was invited by previous emperors but required by Domitian. In any case, the apocalyptic form of Revelation renders the situation less important than the style and content, to which we now turn our attention.

Structure as a Key to Meaning

Because the sequence of events described in its visions overlap, Revelation defies organizational schemes along strictly chronological lines. We noted above the all-important beginning section, the message of Christ to the seven churches (chapters 1–3). Then the close of the present age is depicted in three series of seven events in the symbolic forms of seals, trumpets, and bowls (4–18). The order of the visions, however, is not necessarily the order of events; furthermore, the sequence of presentation is interrupted by a series of signs or portents (12–14). Once these visions are reported, John conveys the future establishment of God's kingdom (19–22) and closes with an assertion of the trustworthiness and inviolability of his message (22:6–21).

Within this structure, Revelation includes several genres in addition to apocalyptic. The entire structure is presented loosely in narrative form, identifying the writer and then setting up the sequence of events he is reporting. The letters to the churches and the personal ending contain style and content familiar from our study of Paul's epistles, and a situation perhaps closest to that of Hebrews, which exhorts persecuted believers to persevere. Scattered throughout Revelation are more than two dozen poems, which are similar in style to poetic portions of the Old Testament prophetic material. Some of these may have been early Christian hymns already in use and incorporated here where they suit the context. So as confusing as the central series of visions may be to a modern audience—and probably to its ancient audience—some aspects of Revelation should be quite familiar to readers of this textbook.

How to Read Revelation

It may be helpful to consider several principles to guide a constructive reading of this fascinating but challenging book. The first is to resist use of Revelation to understand the future in detail. Those who encounter the book through the eyes of faith often experience, or cause, great confusion in this effort. Despite the proposals of many well-meaning interpreters, no one has yet produced a broadly accepted explanation that reconciles Revelation with all the relevant biblical material and current or future events, nor could anyone verify such an explanation until the events have occurred. Hence my advice to the faithful: better to know that one is invited to the party than to know exactly when and where it will take place.

A second principle to help understand Revelation is to understand that visionary material is intended to *evoke*, not to *describe*. For example, the heavenly Jesus is depicted as having a sword coming out of his mouth (1:16) and as a bleeding lamb with seven horns and seven eyes (5:6) who can still open sealed scrolls (6:1) even though he is holding seven stars in one hand (1:16). The point of these texts is not to portray how Christ *looks* in his heavenly state but to convey how the audience should *respond* to these highly evocative but figurative depictions: with wonder, gratitude, and obedience. Similarly figurative is the depiction of heaven as a New Jerusalem (21:2–26) in the form of a gigantic cube filled with jewel-encrusted walls and gates that lands on top of a mountain. A literal rendering is impossible and even a little ridiculous; but as a symbolic depiction of a perfectly ordered community, the message begins to make sense. Applying this logic throughout Revelation, the reader learns to set aside pictures and think instead in terms of responses.

The third principle to guide a reading of Revelation is to understand the focus on the audience's response in the present. The imagery of the future always points back to the current message to the seven churches in chapters 2–3. That is, readers who wonder at God's majesty as revealed in the heavenly court, at God's plan as revealed in the unfolding of events, and at God's love in the figure of the Lamb (Christ) should grow and persevere in their faith as they are admonished in the letters. In this regard, the message of Revelation is neatly aligned with the "little apocalypse" in the Gospels: To anticipate future events is to make oneself ready, and to be ready is not to profess expertise about the future but to live a transformed life.

Imagery and Archetypes in Revelation

Before reading the text of Revelation, it may be helpful to review the description of symbols, archetypal images, and archetypal plots in chapter 9 above. Virtually all of the images in Revelation are abundantly present in the Old Testament, but even the reader who is unfamiliar with the prophetic and wisdom writings—or who has not studied modern psychologists like Freud and Jung—can work out most of the intended responses. Still, with Revelation throwing out every image but the kitchen sink (there were no kitchen sinks then), the challenge is to find an organizing or unifying focus. The myriad images in the book might be viewed in two ways, or at two levels.

The first level of categorization should be to understand images in *opposition*, because it is fundamental to apocalyptic to view the cosmic struggle in dualistic terms of good versus evil or order versus chaos. As we noted in chapter 9, the opposite archetypal image, standing for the opposite value, is implied or understood even if it is not shown in a given passage. Where there is darkness, light must be waiting to break forth. If there is a threatening dragon, there must be a triumphant Lamb. The chaotic sea must give way to the peaceful river. Look for the dualism of good versus evil in colors, light and dark, minerals, sounds, and kinds of creatures. Look for dualism of order versus chaos in grouping of numbers, poetry, repetition, song, shapes, celestial bodies, and natural features like mountains, rivers, and seas.

A second level of categorization is *movement*. Given the linear progression of the entire biblical story, and Revelation as its summary, we should be aware of movements upward and forward for both individuals and events. These are symbolic plot elements, participating in the larger picture of direction toward redemption. So the question is not only "What do these images represent?" but "Where are they going?"

Armed with awareness of the importance of opposition and the sense of movement, a reader can respond to Revelation as one might to an Impressionist painting, or even a modern, nonrepresentational work of art. The novice asks, "What is it?" But the lover of art asks, "How does it make me feel?" or "How does it want me to respond?"

Read Revelation 1–3

23a: Every detail is significant in 2:12–20. Which symbols and archetypes convey what attributes of God?

23b: Although generally the letters to the churches are exhortations to persevere in the face of persecution, they are worded in heavily symbolic language. With either the letter to Sardis or to Laodicea, list the symbolic terms and suggest what each might mean in terms of belief or activity on the part of the audience.

Read Revelation 4–20

23c: Some images in the depiction of the heavenly court (ch 4–5) are not quite moral or ordered but simply grand or mysterious. What are these and what is their function?

23d: What do containers or limiters (unsealed scrolls, blasted trumpet, and emptied bowls) have in common, and what is the combined effect of the quantity and character of these judgments?

Read Revelation 21–22

23e: What symbols and archetypes convey order and moral perfection in the vision of New Jerusalem?

23f: Look in this section for repetition of elements, which we learned from Old Testament texts is a common mechanism to drive home the importance of an idea; what ideas are driven home here?

Image and Message in Revelation

New Testament Themes and Priorities

Unlike the Old Testament, which ends with an expectant tone in the brief prophetic book of Malachi, the New Testament ends with a depiction of history's closure in the lengthy book of Revelation. Interestingly, even the arrangement of books becomes a literary feature. For how different would the overall New Testament message be if the centuries of debate in the early church about including Revelation (largely on the grounds of its obscurity) had gone the other way? Or what if Revelation followed Acts, and the New Testament ended with the epistles? The result of choices made by early Christian councils is a kind of 27-part narrative, from the birth of Jesus to John's vision of heaven, of events that took place over one hundred years, whose authors composed the collection in the second half of that century, but whose themes cover the entire span of human history. What are some of the key themes and priorities of the New Testament?

At its core, the New Testament is a *comedy*. Against impossible odds, despite overwhelming opposition, defying all expectation—the hunted baby lives, the crucified peasant becomes king, the first become last, the underdog wins on a final (and literal!) Hail Mary pass, and the meek inherit the earth. To the extent that modern readers can see beneath the accumulated sludge of religious conflict and oppression brought on by distortion of the original comedic message, they can hear every page of the New Testament hum with anticipation and then chuckle at the joke. The punch line is present in every paradox that reverses human expectation: who is righteous (the humble, the outcast), who is messiah (the nonviolent sufferer, the Lamb), who is powerful (the servant), who triumphs (the poor in spirit, the merciful, the persecuted).

A second dominant theme is that *the new covenant completes the old.* This is part of the linear view of history adopted from the Old Testament, which regards history as a one-way journey toward God's redemption. It is evident in the geographic movement of the Gospels and Acts toward Jerusalem and then out into the world, in the tone of expectation throughout the epistles, and in the culminating visions of Revelation. Theologically, it is also present in Jesus' assertion (and Paul's confirmation) that his work does not end or replace the Old Testament but fulfills it. This is most obvious in the affirmation by both Jesus and Paul of Old Testament morality. It appears more subtly in the depiction of Jesus as a kind of microcosm of the nation: wandering in the wilderness, experiencing the miraculous, practicing righteousness, suffering unjustly, having his "temple" (body) destroyed, then rising from the rubble in triumph.

A third core theme or priority is that *faith produces love.* From Jesus' demands of radical discipleship, through Paul's description of the everyday ethics of freedom and unity, to Revelation's call for perseverance in righteousness despite persecution, the New Testament is an intensely practical collection of writings. Faith does not turn in on itself but turns outward in love, and love is not understood in the New Testament as a feeling of affection but as activity in the service of others. This is the resolution of the conflict between Judaism and Hellenism, between faith and works, between religious leaders and common people: right theology is all well and good, but belief only makes sense as people change and act in love to give, forgive, and build one another up.

Closely related to the notion of faith as a producer of love is the New Testament message that *love produces community.* Lost in English translation is that virtually every behavioral command is addressed to you *plural*, not you *singular*. Important passages that describe relationships within the community include Jesus' "farewell discourse" in John 14–17, the description of the initial group of believers in Acts 2–4, Paul's lengthy treatment of unity in 1 Corinthians, and of course the vision of a symbolic, perfected community at the end of Revelation. But the focus on unity and growth *together* is explicit or implicit on almost every page of the New Testament. Faith does not develop or manifest in isolation but in interaction with others.

It may be unfair to describe the New Testament as a *work of literature* in the conscious sense. Instead, the literary elements reside in particular passages or kinds of writing. New Testament writers intended their work for an illiterate audience who would hear rather than read their words. In most cases they wrote in non-literary Greek and addressed immediate, practical concerns—after all, they did not expect the world to go on for more than a few generations, much less for two thousand years. Nevertheless, at times they wrote with painstaking care for detail, down to the nuances of exact words and even verb tenses, as we see from scrutiny of the differences between the Gospels, or Paul's doctrinal thesis to the Romans, or Hebrews' sophisticated argument for Jesus' importance. We may also observe simple beauty in a parable of Jesus, intriguing tone in his manner of speaking, and high drama as he faces death on trumped-up charges. We observe experimentation with existing literary forms in the epistles and Gospels, and we end the collection with a kaleidoscope of imagery in Revelation. Of course, in order to address real human needs and aspirations, the New Testament *must* be literature. If it was only a list of doctrines and behavioral demands, it would not be *fully human*—which, as Paul might argue, is the only way it could also be *fully divine*.

For Further Study:

1. If the language of Revelation is symbolic, can the situation (eventual judgment, heaven and hell) also be construed as symbolic? How far can logic take the distinction between literal and figurative?

2. Research the idealist, preterist, and futurist interpretive schemes for the application of Revelation to Christian belief; which one, in your view, best represents the original intent and the ongoing significance of the book?

3. Compare any category of symbols to those found in the Old Testament (e.g., heavenly furniture, forms of judgment, creatures, depictions of God). Do these comparisons shed light on the imagery of Revelation?

4. If the evil female figure of chapters 12–14 represents Rome, does the context support the good female figure as Mary, or as the community of believers?

5. Research the significance of the sea as a biblical symbol, and explain why "the sea is no more" in Rev 21:1. Why is a river good and a sea bad?

6. Consider archetypal plots (ch 9) and discuss which best fits Revelation; how does this affect or reflect the overall biblical view of history?

Summing Up

Summing *up* is a fitting title for this final page, because our approach to the Bible as literature demands a progression *up*ward. This is due in part to the strong sense of linear movement toward something better, a Promised Land, Jerusalem built and then rebuilt, a message that travels to Jerusalem and out to the world; finally, the New Jerusalem. There is never a sense in the Bible of going back to the Garden; progress is always forward to a City. Those of us today who love the wilderness and the countryside may find this odd; but then, few of us would last long in our favorite "natural" destination without a smart phone and a cooler full of snacks. The biblical movement does not discount the beauty of the natural world, but it asserts that our movement upward must be away from isolated individuality and toward human community, harmony, and healing. The vision of perfection involves love, which can only be perfected in relation to other people.

Another upward movement that characterizes a literary approach to the Bible is the movement toward a unifying view of its message, which is difficult to find. The naïve approach to the Bible assumes that it contains only a compendium of doctrines and instructions for living, and you either believe or you don't. What we find instead is that one-third of the Bible is poetry; but where we might expect epic poetry to convey developments, we get creative narrative instead. Stories, poems, parables, and prophecies turn out to reveal complex ideas that tease out insight rather than clubbing readers over the head. Further challenges are presented by the diversity of ethical and theological views within and between Old and New Testaments. Where does this all lead? Oliver Wendell Holmes said, "For the simplicity that lies this side of complexity, I would not give a fig, but for the simplicity that lies on the other side of complexity, I would give my life." The challenge to the reader of the Bible, whether that reader comes to the study with a high view of inspiration or merely historical interest, is to move up from those early simplistic assumptions, to face the fascinating but intimidating complexity of the Bible, and then to find some kind of unified and unifying response.

Is this possible? If so, it represents work that lies beyond the scope of this book, but our study may have supplied hints or first steps. For what is the progression from *truth* to *Truth* if not a movement upward? As we saw from the opening chapters, biblical study presents intriguing academic questions regarding authorship, time of writing, and the accuracy or consistency of events and ideas depicted in this collection of writings. But the sum of these parts may represent something altogether different from a pile of facts—or at least, one may stand (unsteadily!) on those facts to reach further up. That is, whether or not one reads the Bible through the lens of faith, one cannot read it without considering the fundamental issues that we all face. Who am I? Does my life have meaning? How do I respond to my own mortality? What connection and responsibility do I have to others? Any serious consideration of these questions that incorporates a work as significant as the Bible is sure to lead to higher ground.

Appendix A

Glossary

acrostic: technique in which the first letters of parts of a poem follow the sequence of the alphabet.

alliteration: repetition of consonants, usually at the beginning of words, in pairs or groups of words grouped closely together.

antithetic parallelism: opposition or contrast of thought in a pair of lines where the second line expresses the truth of the first in a negative way.

apocalyptic: genre characterized by God's victorious intervention in history and reward for the elect following a cosmic struggle.

apocrypha: intertestamental books not included in the canon except by Roman Catholics.

apostle: one of Jesus' original twelve followers; later, an early church missionary.

apostolicity: criterion for inclusion in the New Testament canon that requires authorship by an apostle or an apostle's associate.

archetype: universal symbol, character type, or story line.

amanuensis: writing secretary often responsible for producing, and possibly having a part in composing, a biblical text.

assonance: repetition of vowels in words grouped closely together.

canon: in biblical studies, the group of writings officially designated as Scripture.

chiasm: X-shaped writing structure.

climactic parallelism: when a line partially repeats and advances the thought of the previous line.

contemporary predictive prophecy: when a biblical prophet foretells the near future.

deuterocanonical: describes the secondary but still-inspired status of the Apocrypha for Roman Catholics.

diaspora: Jews who live outside of Palestine.

docetism: the belief that Jesus only seemed human.

documentary hypothesis or *JEDP theory:* explains the composition of the Pentateuch from four distinct sources, which are characterized by distinct styles.

dramatic irony: when information is known to the reader but not to the characters.

epistle: ancient essay formatted as a letter, or a New Testament letter.

eschatological: writings pertaining to the *eschaton* or end of time.

form criticism: the attempt to reconstruct the original situation that produced a piece of writing by studying its final form.

future predictive prophecy: when a biblical prophet foretells the distant future.

Gnosticism: rival thought system to early Christianity influenced by Platonic philosophy that stressed the superiority of spirit over matter.

Gospel: one of the four versions of the life of Jesus: Matthew, Mark, Luke, and John.

gospel: the message of the early Christians concerning salvation.

Hellenism: following Alexander's conquest, the Greek way of life, often in tension with Judaism.

image: names a concrete thing or action where the first level of meaning is primary, and the reader must consider what the image evokes.

interpretive prophecy: when a biblical prophet gives God's perspective on current events.

intertestamental: between Old and New Testaments, c. 450 BC to AD 50.

irony: statement that suggests the opposite of its literal meaning.

Judaizers: opponents of Paul who required strict observance of the Jewish law for Christian converts.

kerygma: the essential message of early Christian preaching.

koine Greek: "common" Greek of the New Testament; the *lingua franca* of the Roman world.

LXX: the Septuagint, the Greek translation of the Old Testament.

Mark-Q documentary hypothesis: accounts for differences and similarities between the Synoptics by maintaining that Mark wrote first, then Matthew and Luke wrote using Mark and separate sources.

Messianic Secret: the gradual revelation of Jesus' identity and mission in the Gospels.

metaphor: comparison in which one term stands for another.

meter: the rhythm of accented syllables in poetry.

myth: a primal story that conveys fundamental insights about reality.

onomatopoeia: use of words that sound like the action they describe.

oracle: in the Bible, a passage that begins, "The word of the Lord."

parable: extended metaphor, sometimes to story length.

parallelism: in biblical poetry, repetition, contrast, or completion of an idea by restatement in the next line.

paronomasia: pun.

Parousia: the second coming of Christ.

patriarch: in the Bible, a father of the nation of Israel: Abraham, Isaac, Jacob, etc.

patriarchal narratives: the biblical account of the patriarchs.

Glossary

Pentateuch: the first five books of the Bible: Genesis, Exodus, Leviticus, Numbers, Deuteronomy.

pericope: a passage in a Gospel; the term is used primarily when comparing differences in accounts.

pseudepigrapha: "falsely inscribed" works, written in the name of a biblical figure.

Q: theoretical source of Jesus' sayings employed by Matthew and Luke.

scribe: in the Bible, an expert on the Jewish law.

scripture: inspired or sacred writing.

Septuagint: the Greek translation of the Old Testament; see LXX.

symbol: names a concrete thing or action where the second level of meaning is primary.

synoptic: in biblical studies, one of the first three Gospels; as a proper name, Synoptic(s).

synthetic parallelism: when one line of a poem completes the thought of the previous line.

synonymous parallelism: similar thought conveyed in successive lines of a poem.

tabernacle: temporary, traveling temple.

Tanakh: another term for the Hebrew Bible or Old Testament, from the three letters T (Torah), N (Nevi'im or prophets), and K (Ketuvim or writings).

typological prophecy: involves the use of a symbol or figure from past writing to interpret current events.

satire: writing that pokes fun at human folly, often using irony and exaggeration.

simile: form of comparison in which one object "is like" another.

testament: in biblical studies, alternately *covenant* or *agreement*, involving promises and obligations between God and humanity.

Torah: the Jewish law, sometimes used for the Pentateuch.

Appendix B

Further Reading and Research

It may surprise the beginning student to learn that the academic study of the Bible is a substantial field involving graduate programs not only at seminaries (training schools for ministers) but at prestigious universities, with thousands of professors who produce mountains of articles and books every year. How is it scholarly to learn a few time-worn interpretations of an ancient book about which nothing new could possibly be said? On the contrary, current methods of analyzing the Bible emerged at the same time as those applied to most other academic disciplines, so the insights are just as new as those discovered for Plato or Shakespeare. Such study may be *more* challenging, in fact, because biblical scholars must master at least five languages and learn about the history, philosophy, comparative literature, and sociology of the ancient world even before they begin to engage in literary interpretation. Biblical study is further complicated by the fact that schools and publishers operate with certain assumptions and conclusions that give them an "editorial policy" like that of a newspaper or television network. While no academic field is free from "politics," the added factor of passionate personal commitment may make the study of religion and of the Bible more prone to fine-tuned bias. Although we might wish for more diversity and objectivity within institutions and publishers, at least this allows the knowledgeable student to choose a school or a book from the myriad choices available with reasonable confidence that it will represent a predictable position.

But given the variety of readers of this text, and the inability of beginning students to identify the range of approaches merely by name of writer, school, or publisher, I must go beyond simple lists in order to offer fair guidance. Within reading lists for each chapter, therefore, I will offer not only titles but also brief comments where it is helpful to indicate where a book lies along the spectrum of scholarly perspectives. I will characterize books as "conservative" that support traditional beliefs about authorship, historical accuracy, and inspiration of biblical books. Those characterized as "middle" or "moderate" tend to support traditional beliefs but sometimes reach nontraditional conclusions about authorship, history, and consistency. Books that I will characterize as "liberal" go furthest in challenging traditional beliefs and will appeal more to a secular or theologically liberal reader. When I do not characterize a book in this manner, the student can assume that it is acceptable across the spectrum.

FURTHER READING AND RESEARCH

Chapter 1: *Approaching the Bible as Literature*: How and Why?

Representative treatments of the Bible as literature:

Alter, Robert. *The Art of Biblical Poetry*. New York: Basic, 1987; also *The Art of Biblical Narrative*. New York: Basic, 1982. Alter's widely-used texts are rich with scholarly insight but may prove challenging for the beginning student of the Bible.

Alter, Robert, ed. *The Literary Guide to the Bible*. Cambridge: Harvard University Press, 1990. This lengthy book-by-book approach includes helpful explanations of the literary features of each biblical book; the perspective of contributors is moderate to liberal.

Crain, Jeanie C. *Reading the Bible as Literature: An Introduction*. Malden, MA: Polity, 2010. This concise guide organizes by type of writing, not chronologically, so it is most useful to those already quite familiar with the Bible. It offers great detail on literary terminology and is especially strong on imagery; the theological perspective is moderate.

Gabel, John B., et al. *The Bible as Literature: An Introduction*. 5th ed. Oxford: University Press, 2006. This general introduction to the Bible and its literary treatment offers a liberal scholarly perspective that challenges traditional beliefs.

Ryken, Leland. *Words of Delight: A Literary Introduction to the Bible*. Grand Rapids: Baker, 1992. This is the most comprehensive of a number of texts written by Ryken on the literary approach to the Bible. He writes from a conservative theological perspective, avoiding issues of authorship or historicity that may trouble some readers; however, he does not assume or demand that readers share his beliefs.

Chapter 2: From Ancient Stories to NRSV: How We Got Here

On the Documentary Hypothesis:

Friedman, Richard Elliott. *The Bible with Sources Revealed*. San Francisco: HarperOne, 2005. This book provides a detailed defense of the documentary hypothesis.

Sailhamer, John H. *The Expositor's Bible Commentary*. Volume 1. *Genesis-Leviticus*. Edited by Tremper Longman III and David E. Garland. Grand Rapids: Zondervan, 2008. The introduction (23–44) provides a moderate alternative to the documentary hypothesis.

On the biblical canon and translations:

Davies, Philip R. *Scribes and Schools: The Canonization of the Hebrew Scriptures*. Louisville: Westminster John Knox, 1998.

Metzger, Bruce. *The Bible in Translation: Ancient and English Versions*. Grand Rapids: Baker, 2001.

———. *The New Testament Canon: Its Origin, Development, and Significance*. Oxford: Clarendon, 1987.

Chapter 3: Truth and truth in the Bible

For C. S. Lewis's pivotal conversation with J.R.R. Tolkien about myth, and for Tolkien's explanation of myth in relation to his own fiction:

Carpenter, Humphrey. *The Inklings*. London: George Allen & Unwin, 1978. Pages 42–43.

———. *The Letters of J. R. R. Tolkien*. Boston: Houghton Mifflin, 1981. Pages 143–61, 252–53.

Hooper, Walter, ed. *The Collected Letters of C. S. Lewis. Vol 1: Family Letters 1905–1931*. San Francisco: Harper, 2003. Pages 969–77.

Tolkien, J. R. R. "On Fairy-Stories." Tolkien, Christopher, ed. *The Monsters and the Critics and Other Essays*. London: George Allen and Unwin, 1983. Pages 109–61.

For a variety of perspectives on the topic of Myth and myth:

Knox, John. *Myth and Truth*. Charlottesville: University of Virginia Press, 1964.

Olson, Alan M., ed. *Myth, Symbol, and Reality*. South Bend: University of Notre Dame Press, 1980.

Chapter 4: The Past Reveals the Present in Genesis 1–11

Primary source material on ancient myths:

Dailey, Stephanie. *Myths from Mesopotamia: Creation, the Flood, Gilgamesh, and Others* Rev. ed. Oxford: University Press, 2009.

Eliade, Mercea. *Gods, Goddesses, and Myths of Creation*. New York: Harper & Row, 1967. Discussion of parallels between biblical and other ancient creation accounts with sensitivity to readers who may regard them as a threat to traditional belief:

Hays, Christopher B. *Hidden Riches: A Sourcebook for the Comparative Study of the Hebrew Bible and Ancient Near East*. Louisville: Westminster John Knox, 2014.

Oswalt, John N. *The Bible Among the Myths: Unique Revelation or Just Ancient Literature?* Grand Rapids: Zondervan, 2009.

Walton, John H. *Ancient Near Eastern Thought and the Old Testament: Introducing the Conceptual World of the Hebrew Bible*. Grand Rapids: Baker Academic, 2009.

Treatments of the early chapters of Genesis in terms of story and theology, not in terms of scientific debate:

Barton, Stephen C., and David Wilkinson, eds. *Reading Genesis after Darwin*. Oxford: Oxford University Press, 2009.

Callender, Dexter E., ed. *Myth and Scripture: Contemporary Perspectives on Religion, Language, and Imagination*. Atlanta: Society of Biblical Literature, 2014.

Good, Edwin M. *Genesis 1–11: Tales of the Earliest World*. Stanford: University Press, 2011.

Gnuse, Robert. *Misunderstood Stories: Theological Commentary on Genesis 1–11*. Eugene, OR: Cascade, 2014.

Chapter 5: Telling the Story Well: Narrative Technique in Genesis and Exodus

Detailed studies about the crafting of biblical stories:

Alter, Robert. *The Art of Biblical Narrative*. New York: Basic, 1981.

Bar-Efrat, Shimon. *Narrative Art in the Bible*. Sheffield Academic Press, 1989.

Fokelman, J. P. *Reading Biblical Narrative: An Introductory Guide*. Louisville: Westminster John Knox, 1999.

Kort, Wesley A. *Story, Text, and Scripture. Literary Interests in Biblical Narrative.* University Park, PA: Pennsylvania State University Press, 1988.

A spectrum of views about the historicity of the biblical account:

Gottwald, Norman K. *The Hebrew Bible: A Brief Socio-Literary Introduction.* Minneapolis: Augsburg Fortress, 2008. This book presents the radical view that Israel's past history was invented in the middle of the first millenium BC.
Finkelstein, Israel and Amihai Mazar. *The Quest for the Historical Israel.* Atlanta: Society of Biblical Literature, 2007. This book summarizes the authors' largely skeptical conclusions about the historicity of the biblical narratives.
Coogan, Michael D. *The Old Testament: A Historical and Literary Introduction to the Hebrew Scriptures.* 2nd ed. Oxford University Press, 2010. A liberal perspective on historicity.
Provan, Iain, V. Phillips Long, and Tremper Longman III. *A Biblical History of Israel.* Louisville: Westminster John Knox, 2003. Three moderately conservative scholars present a case for the general accuracy of the Old Testament historical narratives.
Arnold, Bill T., and Richard S. Hess, eds. *Ancient Israel's History: An Introduction to Issues and Sources.* Grand Rapids: Baker, 2014. Contributions by numerous conservative scholars, with a conservative perspective on historicity.
Hoerth, Alfred. *Archaeology and the Old Testament.* Grand Rapids: Baker, 1998. This well-illustrated, very conservative volume presents archaeological findings as consistently supportive or illustrative of the biblical historical record.

Studies of Genesis and Exodus, with the most conservative listed first:

Wenham, Gordon J. *Genesis.* 2 vols. Nashville: Thomas Nelson, 1987–94.
Hamilton, Victor P. *The Book of Genesis.* 2 Vols. Grand Rapids: Eerdmans, 1995.
Westermann, Klaus. *Genesis.* 3 vols. Minneapolis: Augsburg Fortress, 1986–90.
Stuart, Douglas K. Exodus: *An Exegetical and Theological Exposition of Holy Scripture.* Nashville: Holman Reference, 2006.
Durham, John I. *Exodus.* Nashville: Thomas Nelson, 1987.
Childs, Brevard S. *The Book of Exodus: A Critical, Exegetical Commentary.* Louisville: Westminster John Knox, 1974.

Chapter 6: Narrative from Exodus to Samuel

Studies of the Old Testament historical books; for each book, the most conservative study is listed first:

Wenham, Gordon. *The Book of Leviticus.* Grand Rapids: Eerdmans, 1979.
Hartley, John E. *Leviticus.* Nashville: Thomas Nelson, 1992.
Milgram, Jacob. *Leviticus: A Book of Ritual and Ethics.* Minneapolis: Augsburg Fortress, 2004.

Cole, Dennis R. *Numbers: An Exegetical and Theological Exposition of Holy Scripture*. Nashville: Holman Reference, 2000.
Budd, Philip J. *Numbers*. Nashville: Thomas Nelson, 1984.
Levine, Baruch A. *Numbers*. 2 Vols. New York: Doubleday, 1993, 2000.

Wright, Christopher. *Deuteronomy*. Peabody, MA: Hendricksen, 2003.
Christensen, Duane L. *Deuteronomy*. 2nd ed., 2 vols., Nashville: Thomas Nelson, 2001.
Peterson, Brian Neil. *The Authors of the Deuteronomistic History: Locating a Tradition in Ancient Israel*. Minneapolis: Augsburg Fortress, 2014.

Woudstra, Martin H. *The Book of Joshua*. Grand Rapids: Eerdmans, 1981.
Butler, Trent C. *Joshua*. 2nd ed., 2 vols. Nashville: Thomas Nelson, 2014.
Boling, Robert G., and G. Ernest Wright. *Joshua*. New York: Doubleday, 1982.

Block, Daniel I. and Kenneth A. Matthews. *Judges, Ruth: An Exegetical and Theological Exposition of Holy Scripture*. Nashville: Holman Reference, 1999.
Butler, Trent C. *Judges*. 2 vols. Nashville: Thomas Nelson, 2009.
Sasson, Jack M. *Judges 1–12*. New Haven, CT: Yale University Press, 2014.

Hubbard, Robert L., Jr. *The Book of Ruth*. Grand Rapids: Eerdmans, 1989.
Bush, Frederick W. *Ruth, Esther*. Nashville: Thomas Nelson, 1996.
Schipper, Jeremy. Ruth. New Haven, CT: Yale University Press, 2016.
Bergen, Robert D. *1, 2 Samuel: An Exegetical and Theological Exposition of Holy Scripture*. Nashville: Holman Reference, 1996.

Klein, Ralph W. *1 Samuel*. Nashville: Thomas Nelson, 1989.
Anderson, A. A. *2 Samuel*. Nashville: Thomas Nelson, 1989.
McCarter, P. Kyle, Jr. *1 Samuel*. New York: Doubleday, 1995.
———. *2 Samuel*. New York: Doubleday, 1984.

House, Paul R. *1 & 2 Kings: An Exegetical and Theological Exposition of Holy Scripture*. Nashville: Holman Reference, 1995.
DeVries, Simon J. *1 Kings*. Nashville: Thomas Nelson, 2004.
Hobbs, J. J. *2 Kings*. Nashville: Thomas Nelson, 1986.
Fritz, Volkmar. *1 & 2 Kings*. Minneapolis: Augsburg Fortress, 2003.

Thompson, J. A. *1, 2 Chronicles: An Exegetical and Theological Exposition of Holy Scripture*. Nashville: Holman Reference, 1994.
Braun, Roddy L. *1 Chronicles*. Nashville: Thomas Nelson, 1986.
Klein, Ralph W. *1 Chronicles*. Minneapolis: Augsburg Fortress, 2006.
Dillard, Raymond J. *2 Chronicles*. Nashville: Thomas Nelson, 1988.
Klein, Ralph W. *2 Chronicles*. Minneapolis: Augsburg Fortress, 2012.

Baldwin, Joyce G. *Esther: An Introduction and Commentary*. Downers Grove, IL: InterVarsity, 1984.
Bush, Frederick W. *Ruth and Esther*. Nashville: Thomas Nelson, 1996.
Levenson, Jon D. *Esther*. Louisville: Westminster John Knox, 1997.

Fensham, Charles. *Ezra and Nehemiah*. Grand Rapids: Eerdmans, 1983.
Williamson, H. G. M. *Ezra and Nehemiah*. Nashville: Thomas Nelson, 1985.
Keck, Leander. *The New Interpreter's Bible Commentary: Ezra-Nehemiah, Introduction to Prophetic Literature, Isaiah, Jeremiah, Baruch, Letter of Jeremiah, Lamentations*. Vol. 4. Nashville: Abingdon, 2015.

Chapter 7: From Solomon to the Close of the Old Testament

Treatments of historicity of Israel's history, with the most conservative listed first:

Kaiser, Walter. *A History of Israel*. Nashville: Hollman, 1998.
Moore, Megan Bishop, and Brad E. Kelle. *Biblical History and Israel's Past: The Changing Study of the Bible and History*. Grand Rapids: Eerdmans, 2011.
Herrmann, Siegfried. *A History of Israel in Old Testament Times*. 2nd ed. Philadelphia: Fortress, 1981.
Aharoni, Johanan, et al. *The MacMillan Bible Atlas*. 3rd ed. New York: MacMillan, 1993.

Chapter 8: Principles of Hebrew Poetry

Studies of the Book of Psalms, with the most conservative listed first:

Kidner, Derek. *Psalms*. 2 vols. Downers Grove, IL: InterVarsity, 1973.
Craigie, Peter C. *Psalms 1–50*. Rev. ed. Nashville: Thomas Nelson, 2004.
Tate, Marvin E. *Psalms 51–100*. Nashville: Thomas Nelson, 1991
Allen, Leslie C. *Psalms 101–150*. Rev. ed. Nashville: Thomas Nelson, 2002.
Kraus, Hans Joachim. *Psalms*. 2 vols. Minneapolis: Augsburg Fortress, 1990.

Chapter 9: Imagery in Hebrew Poetry

On biblical imagery, see the books listed for chapter 1 and the following:

Gibson, J. C. L. *Language and Imagery in the Old Testament*. Peabody, MA: Hendrickson, 1998.
Gillingham, S. E. *The Poems and Psalms of the Hebrew Bible*. Oxford: University Press, 1994.
Keel, Othmar. *The Symbols of the Biblical World: Ancient Near Eastern Iconography and the Book of Psalms*. New York: Seabury, 1978.

Chapter 10: From Lament to Praise in the Book of Psalms

See the recommendations for chapters 8-9 for studies of the Book of Psalms.

Chapter 11: The Prophets Speak for God

On ethics and social justice in the Old Testament:

Green, Joel B., and Jacqueline E. Lapsley, eds. *The Old Testament and Ethics: A Book-by-Book Survey*. Grand Rapids: Baker, 2013.

Hiers, Richard H. *Justice and Compassion in Biblical Law*. New York: Continuum, 2009.
Piper, John S. *Love Your Enemies: Jesus' Love Command in the Synoptic Gospels and the Early Christian Paraenesis.* Cambridge University Press, 1981.
Malchow, Bruce V. *Social Justice in the Hebrew Bible*. Collegeville, MN: Liturgical, 1996.

Studies of the prophetic books, in canonical order, with the most conservative listed first:

Oswalt, John N. *The Book of Isaiah*. 2 vols. Grand Rapids: Eerdmans, 1986, 1988.
Watts, John D. W. *Isaiah*. 2 vols. Rev. ed. Nashville: Thomas Nelson, 2004.
Wildberger, Hans. *Isaiah 1–12, Isaiah 13–27, Isaiah 28–39*. 3 vols. Minneapolis: Augsburg Fortress, 1991–2002.
Baltzer, Klaus. *Deutero-Isaiah*. Minneapolis: Augsburg Fortress, 2001.

Thompson, J. A. *A Book of Jeremiah*. Grand Rapids: Eerdmans, 1980.
Craigie, Peter C. *Jeremiah 1–25*. Nashville: Thomas Nelson, 1991.
Keown, Gerald L., Pamela J. Scalise, and Thomas G. Smothers. *Jeremiah 26–52*. Nashville: Thomas Nelson, 1995.
Lundbom, Jack R. *Jeremiah*. 3 vols. New Haven, CT: Yale University Press, 1999, 2004.

Block, Daniel I. *Ezekiel*. 2 vols. Grand Rapids: Eerdmans, 1997, 1998.
Allen, Leslie A. *Ezekiel*. 2 vols. Nashville: Thomas Nelson, 1994.
Zimmerli, Walter. *Ezekiel*. 2 vols. Minneapolis: Augsburg Fortress, 1988.

Baldwin, Joyce G. *Daniel*. Downers Grove, IL: InterVarsity, 1978.
Goldingay, John E. *Daniel*. Nashville: Thomas Nelson, 1989.
Collins, John J. *Daniel*. Minneapolis: Augsburg Fortress, 1994.

McComiskey, Thomas E. *Minor Prophets*. 3 vols. Grand Rapids: Baker Academic, 1992.
Stuart, Douglas. *Hoseah-Jonah*. Nashville: Thomas Nelson, 1987.
Smith, Ralph. *Micah-Malachi*. Nashville: Thomas Nelson, 1984.
Keck, Leander. *The New Interpreter's Bible Commentary: The Twelve Prophets, Volume 7*. Nashville: Abingdon, 1996.

Chapter 12: Pondering Imponderables in Wisdom Literature

On literary aspects of the wisdom writings:

Alter, Robert. *The Art of Biblical Poetry*. New York: Basic, 1987. The sections on Job and Song of Songs are particularly helpful.
Fox, Michael. *The Song of Songs and Ancient Egyptian Love Poetry*. Madison: University of Wisconsin, 1985.
Williams, James G. *Those Who Ponder Proverbs: Aphoristic Thinking and Biblical Literature*. Sheffield: University Press, 1981.

Studies of the wisdom writings, in canonical order, with the most conservative listed first:

Andersen, Francis I. *Job*. Downers Grove, IL: InterVarsity Academic, 2009.
Clines, David A. *Job*. 3 vols. Nashville: Thomas Nelson, 1989–2011.

Dhorme, Edouard. *A Commentary on the Book of Job*. Nashville: Thomas Nelson, 1967.

Waltke, Bruce. *Proverbs*. 2 vols. Grand Rapids: Eerdmans, 2005.
Murphy, Roland E. *Proverbs*. Nashville: Thomas Nelson, 1998.
Scott, R. B. Y. *Proverbs and Ecclesiastes*. New York: Doubleday, 1965.

Longman, Tremper. *Ecclesiastes*. Grand Rapids: Eerdmans, 1997,
Murphy, Roland E. *Ecclesiastes*. Nashville: Thomas Nelson, 1998.
Seow, Choon-Leong. *Ecclesiastes*. Yale: University Press, 1997.

Longman, Tremper. *Song of Songs*. Grand Rapids: Eerdmans, 2001.
Garrett, Duane and Paul R. House. *Song of Songs and Lamentations*. Nashville: Thomas Nelson, 2004.
Murphy, Roland. *The Song of Songs*. Minneapolis: Augsburg Fortress, 1990.

On themes and priorities in the Old Testament:

Brueggemann, Walter. *Theology of the Old Testament: Testimony, Dispute, Advocacy*. Minneapolis: Augsburg Fortress, 1997.
Routledge, Robin. *Old Testament Theology: A Thematic Approach*. Downers Grove, IL: InterVarsity, 2008.

Chapter 13: The View from the Bridge

On the intertestamental period, especially for background of the New Testament:

Green, Joel B., and Lee Martin McDonald. *The World of the New Testament*: Cultural, Social, and Historical Contexts. Grand Rapids: Baker Academic, 2013.
Jeremias, Joachim. *Jerusalem in the Time of Jesus*. Philadelphia: Fortress, 1969.
Koester, Helmut, *History, Culture, and Religion of the Hellenistic Age*. Volume 1. New York: Walter de Gruyter, 1995.
Reicke, Bo. *The New Testament Era*. Philadelphia, Fortress, 1968.
Simon, Marcel. *Jewish Sects in the Time of Jesus*. Philadelphia: Fortress, 1967.

Chapter 14: Old Testament Plus

On apocalyptic literature:

Collins, John J. *The Apocalyptic Imagination: An Introduction to Jewish Apocalyptic Literature*. 2nd ed. Grand Rapids: Eerdmans, 1998.
Russell, D. S. *The Method and Message of Jewish Apocalyptic: 200 BC–AD 100*. Philadelphia: Westminster, 1964.
Sacchi, Paolo. *Jewish Apocalyptic and its History*. Sheffield: Sheffield Academic Press, 1990.

Chapter 15: One Story, Four Versions

Studies of the Gospels, in canonical order, with the most conservative listed first:

Carson, Donald A. *Matthew: Expositor's Bible Commentary, Volume 8*. Grand Rapids: Zondervan, 1989.
Davies, W. D., and Dale C. Allison. *Matthew*. 3 Vols. Edinburgh: T. & T. Clark, 1988–97.
Albright, W. F., and C. S. Mann. *Matthew*. New Haven, CT: Yale University Press, 1995.

Lane, William. *The Gospel of Mark*. Grand Rapids: Eerdmans, 1974.
Guelich, Robert A. *Mark*. 2 vols. Nashville: Thomas Nelson, 1989.
Marcus, Joel. *Mark*. 2 vols. New Haven, CT: Yale University Press, 2002, 2009.

Bock, Darrell L. *Luke*. 2 vols. Grand Rapids: Baker, 1996.
Nolland, John. *Luke*. 3 vols. Nashville: Thomas Nelson, 1989–93.
Fitzmyer, Joseph A. *The Gospel according to Luke*. 2 Vols. New York: Doubleday, 1982–85.

Carson, Donald A. *The Gospel according to John*. Grand Rapids: Eerdmans, 1990.
Brown, Raymond. *The Gospel according to John*. 2 vols. New York: Doubleday, 1966–70.
Malina, Bruce J., and Richard L. Rohrbaugh. *Social Science Commentary on the Gospel of John*. Minneapolis: Augsburg Fortress, 1998.

Chapter 16: Jesus According to Matthew

See the recommendations for chapter 15 for studies of the Gospel of Matthew.

Chapter 17: Principles in Parables

On the parables:

Blomberg, Craig. L. *Interpreting the Parables*. Downers Grove, IL: InterVarsity, 1990.
Jeremias, Joachim. *The Parables of Jesus*. New York: Scribners, 1963.
Longenecker, Richard N. *The Challenge of Jesus' Parables*. Grand Rapids: Eerdmans, 2000.

Chapter 18: Parables of Kingdom and Discipleship

See the recommendations for chapter 17 for studies on the parables.

Chapter 19: The Epistle and Community Construction

See the recommendations for chapter 1 for literary features of the epistles.

Chapter 20: A Brief History of Early Christianity

On the historicity of Acts and the beginnings of Christianity:

Bruce, F. F. *New Testament History.* New York: Doubleday, 1980.
Hengel, Martin. *Acts and the History of Earliest Christianity.* Philadelphia: Fortress, 1979.
Witherington, Ben III. *New Testament History: A Narrative Account.* Grand Rapids: Baker, 2003.

Studies of on the Book of Acts, with the most conservative listed first:

Bock, Darrell. *Acts.* Grand Rapids: Baker, 2007.
Fitzmyer, Joseph A. *Acts of the Apostles.* New Haven, CT: Yale University Press, 1998.
Haenchen, Ernst. *The Acts of the Apostles: A Commentary.* Minneapolis: Augsburg Fortress, 1971.

In a blatant act of self-promotion, I also recommend:

Schmidt, Thomas. *The Apostles after Acts: A Sequel.* Eugene, OR: Cascade, 2013. This book reconstructs a hypothetical third volume by Luke; based on historical sources and research, it traces the activities of the Twelve and other important New Testament figures into the late decades of the first century.

Chapter 21: Style and Content in the Epistles

Studies of the New Testament epistles, in canonical order, with the most conservative listed first:

Moo, Douglas. *The Epistle to the Romans.* Grand Rapids: Eerdmans, 1996.
Dunn, James D. G. *Romans.* 2 vols. Nashville: Thomas Nelson, 1988.
Cranfield, C. E. B. *Romans.* 2 vols. Edinburgh: T. & T. Clark, 2000.

Fee, Gordon. *The First Epistle to the Corinthians.* Rev. ed. Grand Rapids: Eerdmans, 2014.
Fitzmyer, Joseph A. *First Corinthians.* New Haven, CT: Yale University Press, 2008.
Conzelmann, Hans. *First Corinthians.* Minneapolis: Augsburg Fortress, 1988.

Hughes, Philip. *The Second Epistle to the Corinthians.* Grand Rapids: Eerdmans, 1962.
Martin, Ralph P. *2 Corinthians.* 2nd ed. Nashville: Thomas Nelson, 2014.

Furnish, Victor Paul. *II Corinthians*. New Haven, CT: Yale University Press, 2005.

Fung, Ronald. *The Epistle to the Galatians*. Grand Rapids: Eerdmans, 1988.
Longenecker, Richard. *Galatians*. Nashville: Thomas Nelson, 1990.
Betz, Hans Dieter. *Galatians*. Minneapolis: Augsburg Fortress, 1979.

O'Brien, Peter T. *Ephesians*. Grand Rapids: Eerdmans, 1999.
Lincoln, Andrew. *Ephesians*. Nashville: Thomas Nelson, 1990.
Barth, Marcus. *Ephesians*. 2 Vols. New Haven, CT: Yale University Press, 1974.

O'Brien, Peter T. *Philippians*. Grand Rapids: Eerdmans, 2014.
Hawthorne, Gerald F. *Philippians*. Rev. ed. Nashville: Thomas Nelson, 2004.
Reumann, John. *Philippians*. New Haven, CT: Yale University Press, 2008.

Moo, Douglas. *The Letters to the Colossians and Philemon*. Grand Rapids: Eerdmans, 2008.
O'Brien, Peter T. *Colossians, Philemon*. Nashville: Thomas Nelson, 1982.
Lohse, Eduard. *Colossians and Philemon*. Minneapolis: Augsburg Fortress, 1988.

Morris, Leon. *The First and Second Epistles to the Thessalonians*. Grand Rapids: Eerdmans, 1984.
Bruce, F. F. *1 & 2 Thessalonians*. Nashville: Thomas Nelson, 1982.
Malherbe, Abraham J. *Letters to the Thessalonians*. New Haven, CT: Yale University Press, 2000.

Mounce, William D. *Pastoral Epistles*. Nashville: Thomas Nelson, 2000.
Knight, George W. *Commentary on the Pastoral Epistles*. Grand Rapids: Eerdmans, 1992.
Conzelmann, Hans, and Martin Dibelius. *The Pastoral Epistles*. Minneapolis: Augsburg Fortress, 1989.

Bruce, F. F. *The Epistle to the Hebrews*. Revised edition. Grand Rapids: Eerdmans, 1990.
Lane, William. *Hebrews*. 2 vols. Nashville: Thomas Nelson, 1991, 1988.
Attridge, Harold. *Hebrews*. Minneapolis: Augsburg Fortress, 1989.

Blomberg, Craig A., and Mariam J. Campbell. *James*. Grand Rapids: Zondervan, 2008.
Martin, Ralph J. *James*. Thomas Nelson, 1988.
Dibelius, Martin, and Martin Greeven. *James*. Minneapolis: Augsburg Fortress, 1988.

Kistemaker, Simon. *Exposition of the Epistles of Peter and Jude*. Grand Rapids: Baker, 1987.
Michaels, J. Ramsey. *1 Peter*. Nashville: Thomas Nelson, 2010.
Baukham, Richard. *Jude, 2 Peter*. Nashville: Thomas Nelson, 1983.

Marshall, I. Howard. *The Epistles of John*. Grand Rapids: Eerdmans, 1978.
Brown, Raymond. *Epistles of John*. New Haven, CT: Yale University Press, 1995.
Strecker, George. *The Johannine Letters*. Minneapolis: Augsburg Fortress, 1996.

Chapter 22: Apocalyptic and Prophecy in the New Testament

See recommendations for chapters 1 and 14 for studies of the apocalyptic genre.

On the role of prophets in the New Testament:

Grudem, Wayne. *The Gift of Prophecy in the New Testament and Today*. Westchester, IL: Crossway, 1988.
Guy, H. A. *New Testament Prophecy: Its Origin and Significance*. London: Epworth, 1947.
Hill, David. *New Testament Prophecy*. Atlanta: John Knox, 1979.

Chapter 23: Image and Message in Revelation

Studies of the Book of Revelation, with the most conservative listed first:

Beale, G. K. *Revelation*. Grand Rapids: Eerdmans, 1998.
Aune, David. *Revelation*. Nashville: Thomas Nelson, 1997,
Fiorenza, Elizabeth Schussler. *The Book of Revelation: Justice and Judgment*. Minneapolis: Augsburg Fortress, 1985.

On New Testament themes:

Bruce. F. F. *The New Testament Development of Old Testament Themes*. Grand Rapids: Eerdmans, 1968.
deSilva, David A. *New Testament Themes*. St. Louis: Chalice, 2001.
Dunn, James D. G. *New Testament Theology: An Introduction*. Nashville: Abingdon, 2009.

Subject Index

Note: This index includes only the names of biblical books given extended treatment; others may be found by following the workbook's generally canonical sequence of material.

acrostic, 51
Acts of the Apostles, 10, 113, 119, 151–53, 154, 179, 195
alliteration, 50–51
allusion, 30, 116, 127, 130, 131
amanuensis, 149
anoint, 39, 89, 102
apocalyptic, 66, 101, 102, 103–5, 167–78, 193, 197
apocrypha, apocryphal, 5, 10, 100–101, 105, 122
apostolicity, 10–11
archetype, 31, 57–60, 77, 78, 174–75, 178, 180
assonance, 51

Bible, authorship, 5, 8–11, 61, 69, 79, 85, 111–14, 148, 149, 151, 154, 161, 162, 164, 172, 181, 186
    date of writing, 5
    historicity, 4, 6, 9–10, 13–16, 75, 187, 189
    history, 38–39, 43–46, 68–69, 95–99, 151–53, 190–93, 195
    literature, as, 3, 5–7, 15–16, 30–32, 49–53, 56–60, 66–70, 79–80, 85, 88–89, 110–15, 121–23, 135–38, 147–49, 169–75, 187
    translation, 11–12, 50, 57, 100, 121, 124

canon, 5, 10–11, 61, 100, 105, 122, 187
character, 9, 13, 26, 29–31, 32, 35, 37, 39, 41, 43, 46, 58, 59, 80, 91, 115, 136
chiasm, 30
Christianity, 10, 99, 101, 112, 148, 151–53, 157, 195
comedy, 31, 59, 115, 179
conflict, 37, 42, 50
contextual proximity, 121–23
covenant, 4, 38, 58, 89, 90, 179
covenant, Abrahamic, 29

Dead Sea Scrolls, 97, 102, 103, 105, 122, 123
deuterocanonical, 100
diaspora, 45, 95, 98

docetism, 162
documentary hypothesis, 9–11, 187

Ecclesiastes, Book of, 87–88, 193
epistle, 10, 101, 145–65, 170, 173, 179–80
eschaton, eschatology, 103, 169–71
Essene, 96, 99, 103, 122

foreshadowing, 30, 118, 127, 153
form criticism, 149, 150

Galatians, Paul's Epistle to the, 154–56, 161, 196
gender, divine, 57
Genesis, Book of, 9, 19–35, 188–189
genre, 7, 30, 109, 148, 169, 172
Gilgamesh, Epic of, 28, 188
Gnostic, Gnosticism, 152, 162, 163, 165
gospel, 151, 157
Gospels, 7, 10, 104–131, 135, 149, 161, 169–70, 174, 179, 194

Hasmonean, 96–97, 99, 101, 103, 193
Hellenism, 96, 99, 101, 102, 105, 114, 179, 193

image, imagery, 30, 50, 56–60, 64, 69, 73, 77, 78, 87, 88, 114, 172, 174–75, 177, 180, 191
inspiration, 6, 10, 14, 32, 105, 122, 181
intertestamental period, 99, 100, 103, 169, 193
irony, 30, 75
    dramatic, 31, 42, 79, 128
Isaiah, Book of, 65–74, 192

James, Epistle of, 147, 149, 154, 161, 164, 196
JEDP, see documentary hypothesis
Job, Book of, 10, 59, 79–84, 91, 192–93
John, 1 Epistle of, 162–63, 164, 170, 196
Jonah, Book of, 75–77, 138, 192
Judaizers, 154

199

Judaism, 38, 79, 91, 96, 98–99, 102, 111, 116, 165
judge, 39
justice, 68–69

kerygma, 151
Ketuvim, 10
koine (Greek), 96

Law, biblical, 9–10, 29, 38, 45, 49, 54, 79, 88, 89, 95, 96, 98, 99, 103, 112, 124, 125, 152, 154, 165
law, natural, 157
Lewis, C.S., 14, 187–88
lingua franca, 96
LXX, see Septuagint

Mark-Q documentary hypothesis, 110
Matthew, Gospel of, 70, 95, 109–12, 116–32, 137, 139, 194
messiah, 10, 43, 67, 77, 89, 90, 103, 104, 110, 112, 113, 114, 116, 118, 127, 152, 170, 179
Messianic Secret, 110, 135
metaphor, 30, 56–57, 60, 77, 135–36
meter, 50, 51, 55
mirroring, see reflective
myth, 13–15, 22–24, 28, 60

narrative technique, 8, 13, 19–46, 56, 57, 67, 68, 77, 78, 91, 110, 111, 115, 116, 118, 128, 129, 132, 136, 138, 144, 181, 188
Nevi'im, 10
New Testament themes, 179–80, 197

Old Testament themes, 90–91, 193
onomatopoeia, 51
oracle, 66
parable, 7, 15–16, 57, 75, 89, 96, 111, 133–44, 194–95
parallelism, 51–63, 74, 85–90
 antithetic, 52
 climactic, 53
 synonymous, 52
 synthetic, 53
paronomasia, 51
Parousia, 164
patriarch, 29, 31–37, 59, 78, 91, 135
pattern, 30
Pentateuch, 9–10, 29, 61, 66, 68, 79, 96, 112, 189–190
pericope, 110
Pharisee, 96, 99, 124, 138, 143, 152, 165
poetry, 16, 29, 31, 47–94, 101, 102, 114, 173, 174, 181, 187, 191–92
plot, 9, 31, 57, 59–60, 174, 180

prophecy, 66, 89–90, 112, 127, 170, 172, 197
 interpretive, 69, 170
 predictive, 69, 169–170, 171
 typological, 69–70, 89, 116
prophet, 39, 43, 66, 118, 135, 171
prophetic writings, 5, 10, 29, 51, 60, 66–78, 89–90, 101, 102, 103, 115, 173, 192
Proverbs, Book of, 85–86, 192–193
psalms, kinds of, 61
Psalms, Book of, 10, 47–65, 70, 76, 79, 89, 90, 91, 131, 191
pseudepigrapha, 10, 102, 105, 122, 169, 170
pun, see word play

Q source, 110
Qumran, see Dead Sea Scrolls

reflective, see mirroring
repetition, 30, 50, 51, 55, 162, 174, 178
Revelation, Book of, 5, 11, 103, 167–180, 197
Romans, Paul's letter to the, 148–49, 154–60, 161, 165, 195

Samaritans, 15, 96, 137, 141, 144
Samuel, Books of, 39–43, 190
Sadducee, 96, 99, 103
satire, 75
scribe, 95, 124
scripture, definition, 5
Septuagint, 100, 122
setting, 13, 31, 129, 136, 144
simile, 30, 56–57, 136
Song of Solomon, 88–89, 192–93
storytelling, see narrative
symbol, symbolic, 21, 31, 56–59, 69, 77, 88, 116, 127, 129, 130, 169, 170, 172–78, 180, 191
synagogue, 96, 99, 117
synoptic, 110, 114, 115, 137, 169, 170

tabernacle, 38
Tanakh, 10
temple, 10, 43, 45, 58, 61, 89, 95, 98–99, 127, 141, 153, 170
testament, 4
Tolkien, J.R.R., 14, 187–88
Torah, see law
tragedy, 31, 39, 41, 43, 59, 111, 115
type, see prophecy, typological

wisdom writings, 79–89, 91, 101–4, 192
word play, 51, 148, 164

www.ingramcontent.com/pod-product-compliance
Lightning Source LLC
Chambersburg PA
CBHW062138160426
43191CB00014B/2318